50 Hikes in

MOUNT RAINIER
NATIONAL PARK

50 Hikes in
MOUNT RAINIER NATIONAL PARK

Third Edition

Text: Ira Spring and Harvey Manning
Photos: Bob and Ira Spring

THE MOUNTAINEERS • SEATTLE
with
The Mount Rainier Natural History
Association

THE MOUNTAINEERS: Organized 1906 ". . . to explore, study, preserve, and enjoy the natural beauty of the Northwest."

Published by The Mountaineers
1011 S.W. Klickitat Way, Suite 107, Seattle, WA 98134

Published simultaneously in Canada by Douglas & McIntyre, Ltd.
1615 Venables Street, Vancouver, B.C. V5L 2H1

Published simultaneously in Great Britain by Cordee
3a DeMontfort St., Leicester, England LE1 7HD

Manufactured in the United States of America
First edition, June 1969
Second edition, June 1978; second printing, October 1980;
third printing, March 1982; fourth printing, July 1983; fifth printing, August 1984; sixth printing April 1986
Third edition, July 1988

7   6   5
8   7   6

Edited by Cathy Johnson
Maps by Marge Mueller
Cover: Edith Creek and Mt. Rainier
Frontispiece: Tatoosh Range from Faraway Rock

Library of Congress Cataloging in Publication Data

Spring, Ira.
    50 hikes in Mount Rainier National Park / authors, Ira Spring and
Harvey Manning ; photos, Bob and Ira Spring ; maps, Marge Mueller. -
- 3rd ed.
        p.   cm.
    Includes index.
    ISBN 0-89886-175-6 (pbk.) :
    1. Hiking--Washington (State)--Mount Rainier National Park--Guide
-books.   2. Mount Rainier National Park (Wash.)--Guide-books.
I. Manning, Harvey.   II. Title.   III. Title: Fifty hikes in Mount
Rainier National Park.   IV. Title: Mount Rainier National Park.
GV199.42.W22M682 1988
917.97'78--dc 19

BRENTANO'S

SALE   5036   104   7658   11-06-95
            REL   3.5   46   12:23:37

                                     10.95
01 0898861756   10.95
            SUBTOTAL   .90
WASHINGTON 8.2% TAX
            TOTAL   11.85
4128002210102161 VISA   11.85
        PV# 0047658

BOOKS MAKE THE GREATEST GIFTS

===========CUSTOMER RECEIPT===========

Aerial view of Columbia Crest and the Emmons Glacier

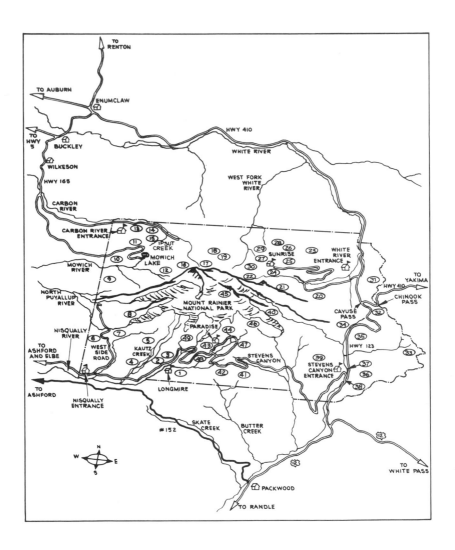

CONTENTS

Air view of Mount Rainier, Pinnacle Peak, center, and The Castle (peak), right

FOREWORD

One of the best ways to savor Mount Rainier is from the trails. You can see the mountain from many different angles and discover its moods and disguises. The peak is like an old-fashioned kaleidoscope. It looks like a different mountain from one side to another. The more you see of it, the more its variety will impress you. You will soon know why native Americans held the peak in such awe and why Northwest citizens all claim it as their own.

We hope you will take some hikes and discover some personal places. For those of you who don't have the time to hike the entire 300 miles of trail in the Park, **50 Hikes in Mount Rainier National Park** will give you a chance to decide which hikes are best for you. There are many new views of the mountain awaiting you around the next bend in the trail, as well as new flower fields, waterfalls, glaciers, deep forests, and perhaps an elusive mountain goat. Take the trail of your choice and discover your own Mount Rainier. Good hiking!

1988
Neal J. Guse, Superintendent
Mount Rainier National Park

Avalanche lilies at Spray Park

INTRODUCTION

The National Park Act of 1916 declares that the purpose of Mount Rainier National Park is "to conserve the scenery and the natural and historic objects and the wildlife... " Each visitor must therefore enjoy the Park "in such manner and by such means as will leave it unimpaired for the enjoyment of future generations." A good motto for Park users is: "Take only pictures. Leave nothing."

The first National Parks were set aside in an era when frontier country was being recklessly exploited by "today" men equally unaware of yesterday and tomorrow. Even then, however, when empty lands seemed inexhaustible, some Americans recognized that certain climaxes of the scenery were too precious to be left open to wanton desecration; thus it was, in 1899, that Mount Rainier National Park was established.

Now, as in the beginning of the concept, a National Park is the highest protection Americans give their land, the purest expression of a nature-sensitive ethic. Ultimately, the ecological conscience must be extended to all remaining wildlands in this nation and every other—and indeed to the entire rural and suburban and urban world. In the National Parks a citizenry still retaining many habits of the frontier can learn the sort of behavior required on a planet that has more people and a more violent technology each passing year.

More Information

All trails in this book are administered by the National Park Service. For further information write:

Mount Rainier National Park; Tahoma Woods, Star Route, Ashford, Washington 98304

Or call:

(206) 569-2211

Trails

Most of the trails in Mount Rainier National Park were built over 50 years ago by people in a hurry to get somewhere, and they vary from steep to very steep. There are three types:

1. *Designated trails,* which comprise the majority of the Park's trails, are the only ones described in this book. These trails were designed and/or built by the Park Service and are marked on maps and signed. Except for a few seldom-used miles, they are exceptionally well maintained.

2. *Way trails* are boot-beaten paths that may be minimally maintained to prevent excessive environmental damage but were not built or designed by the Park Service and are not marked on maps or signed.

3. *Social trails* are made by people taking shortcuts across meadows. The Park Service spends a lot of its resources rehabilitating meadows damaged by social trails.

On the whole, the Park has the best-built and best-maintained trails of any area in Washington, offering many miles of wide, smooth paths.

Conditions are especially good in forests; in alpine meadows, where the short season makes maintenance difficult, the tread is sometimes sketchy.

As soon as the snow melts, trail crews cut away fallen trees and repair winter damage. River crossings are the worst problem. The glacial streams flood and change course and wash out bridges with exasperating frequency. Much of the flooding occurs in June, and it may be mid-July before all the bridges are replaced. If planning a hike before that date, be sure to find out at a Park entrance or ranger station whether the necessary bridges are in place.

Memorial Day is the target date to replace bridges lost during spring floods and to put the walking boards back on the suspension bridges. In addition to the lack of bridges, early season hikers may encounter major tree blowdowns blocking trails. May and June are notorious for late avalanches that often plunge far below the normal snowlines. Trails above 4000 feet may be hidden under 10 feet of snow until July, making navigation difficult in good weather and darn near impossible in a fog. Prior to July and after mid-September, hikers are advised to carry ice axes.

The Mount Rainier contour maps in both the 15-minute and 7½-minute series, as well as in the Green Trails version (available for purchase at map stores and the Park's visitor centers) should be carried and consulted by any party taking a long trip. An accurate lithographed pictorial map of the Park, painted by Dee Molenaar from 1960 aerial photographs, is also available.

Pets

Mount Rainier trails are for people and for the animals who live there. **Pets are not allowed on any trail in the Park.** Wildlife quickly disappears when a dog starts sniffing around—except, maybe, a bear who is angered by the barking and thus becomes a danger to people. The rule against pets covers even the smallest dog or cat, pets on leash, pets carried in arms, and pets walking to one side of the trail and thus technically "not on it." There are no boarding kennels in the Park, so pets should be left at home.

Dogs bother not only wild animals but tame people as well. Most complaints come from hikers who have been harassed by noisy dogs or have found excrement in their assigned campsites. Rangers are required to give a citation whenever a dog is found in the backcountry.

Horses are allowed on a few trails in the Park, but their impact on the terrain requires careful management. A party wishing to travel by horse must contact Park headquarters at Ashford to check on the trails that are open to horse use before the trip.

Clothing

Street shoes and city clothing are fine for nature walks and short forest trails, but any long trip—especially at high altitudes—calls for something better. (Hikers arriving at Mount Rainier without proper gear can rent boots from the guide service at Paradise.)

Sturdy, lug-soled boots are essential for safety and enjoyment on slippery mud and snow, of which Rainier has its share.

Anyone hiking more than an hour from the road must give careful thought to clothing—and the weather. A clear morning is no guarantee it won't be raining by noon, and though being soaked an hour's walk from a dry car is a minor misery in the lowlands, above treeline the experience can be serious.

Mount Rainier makes its own weather, often in a hurry and without warning. Warm sunshine may give way in minutes to a cold, damp fog, and in minutes more to driving rain or snow. A person clothed only for sunshine should turn around and head for home at the first sign of changing weather. Better yet, of course, is to be prepared for the worst by carrying a pack containing a sweater and a hooded windbreaker, raincoat or poncho, and rain pants or chaps.

There is no way to stay dry while hiking in a heavy rain. The maximum hope is to shed some of the water and meanwhile keep warm. Waterproof garments hold the rain out and the perspiration in—the hiker gets wet from the inside. No matter how high the price or how extravagant the advertising claims, the "miracle" fabrics may indeed let the sweat "breathe out," but after a few hours in a downpour, they let the rain leak in. When wearing waterproof or water-repellent garments, it is wise to slow down to avoid overheating.

Some prefer to hike in shorts and T-shirts, getting sopping wet but maintaining warmth by moving at a steady pace; at camp they then put on dry clothing from the pack. If—and only if—one has the dry clothing, this is a good method, especially on overnight trips, but makes for a lot of shivering during rest-stops.

The best solution for most circumstances is to wear wool clothing (trousers and shirt) which provides warmth even when wet. However, backpacker shops offer a variety of high-tech, high-priced alternatives to wool—garments bubbled out of a chemist's pot and painted up as pretty as butterflies.

The need for plenty of warm clothing when hiking above treeline cannot be stressed too much. There have been more fatalities in the Park from exposure leading to hypothermia (subnormal body temperature) than from climbing accidents. Wind and wet weather on simple and easy trails have killed more people than icefalls.

A study by the U.S. Army Surgeon General shows a wind speed of 15 miles per hour and a temperature of 67° (which should be considered fairly "balmy" conditions in Mount Rainier meadows) are as chilling as a still-air temperature of 23°. Even in midsummer, Mount Rainier hikers often encounter 35-mile-per-hour winds and 39° temperatures—the "chill equivalent" of a still-air −38°. The combination of wind and rain or snow is even more lethal.

Hypothermia is insidious in the way it creeps up unrecognized; experienced mountaineers are caught almost as often as beginners. By the time a person realizes he is not merely weary, shivering, sluggish, and awkward of body and mind, but is suffering from hypothermia, he may have no strength left to save himself. Indeed, the mind typically becomes too dulled to be aware of danger. The victim sinks to the ground to rest "for just a minute" and slips unaware into a final sleep.

(Overleaf) Mt. Adams, center, Mt. Hood, right, Tatoosh Range in foreground, as seen from the south side of Mt. Rainier

The lesson is obvious: a person who lacks sufficient clothing, shelter, and food should start for safety at first hint of bad weather—going back to the car, or at least down to timberline.

Other Equipment

Proper boots and clothing, plus perhaps a sandwich or candy bar stuffed in the pocket, suffice for the shorter and easier Mount Rainier hikes. The longer and more complicated trips demand the fuller outfit discussed in **Mountaineering: The Freedom of the Hills** (see "Recommended Reading").

From years of experience, some of it tragic, The Mountaineers have developed a list of items that should be carried by every person on any extended walk—items which provide the minimum conditions for survival when an accident or loss of route or sudden storm makes the trip longer or more severe than expected. Every person should carry these **Ten Essentials**—some in the pockets, others in the rucksack.

1. Extra clothing
2. Extra food. (The test: is there something left over at the end of the trip?)
3. Sunglasses. (Without them even a short snow crossing can be uncomfortable; prolonged snow travel can damage the eyes.)
4. Knife. (A simple pocket variety is enough; uses include first aid and emergency fire-building.)
5. Matches. (Waterproof or in a waterproof container.)
6. Firestarter. (Chemical fuels, easy burning, for starting an emergency fire with wet wood.)
7. First aid kit
8. Flashlight
9. Map
10. Compass

Camping and Fires

Camping is the most damaging of all uses of fragile alpine meadows and if not carefully controlled quickly turns them into dustbowls.

To preserve highland gardens the Park Service has initiated a back-country use-permit system.

Backcountry permits are free and are required for camping at any time of the year. They may be obtained for specific campsites at any ranger station during regular business hours on a first-come first-served basis.

In addition to permits for designated camps, off-trail ("cross-country") permits are issued to give the experienced hiker a chance for solitude. Wood fires are banned at all camps and from all off-trail camping.

Some of the designated camps have small open-end shelter cabins. The shelters are available on a first-come first-served basis; since they hold only three or four people comfortably, most campers carry a plastic tarp or a lightweight alpine tent.

The bough bed, beloved of the frontier past, entails so much damage to vegetation that it is obsolete in many areas, including all National Parks. In Mount Rainier National Park, **one must never cut boughs for a bed.** Instead, carry an air mattress or a foam-plastic pad.

The wood fire, another age-old camping tradition, is also obsolete in Mount Rainier high country. At best, dry firewood is hard to find at popular camps; the easy wood was burnt years ago. What remains now is largely from picturesque silver snags and down logs that are an integral part of the alpine scenery. In using such material, and even more so in cutting branches from living trees (**strictly illegal,** and they don't burn anyway), one erodes the very beauty that made the hike worth taking.

The Mountaineers strongly urge alpine hikers to carry a lightweight stove for cooking and to depend on clothing and shelter (and evening strolls) for warmth. The pleasures of a roaring blaze on a cold mountain night are indisputable, but for the sake of these pleasures a single party on a single night may use up elements of the scenery that were long decades in growing, dying, and silvering.

Water

Hikers traditionally have drunk the water in wilderness in confidence, doing their utmost to avoid contaminating it so the next person also can safely drink. But there is no assurance your predecessor has been so careful.

No open water ever, nowadays, can be considered safe for human consumption. Any reference in this book to "drinking water" is not a guarantee. It is entirely up to the individual to judge the situation and decide whether to take a chance.

In the late 1970s began a great epidemic of giardiasis, caused by a vicious little parasite that spends part of its life cycle swimming free in water, part in the intestinal tract of beavers and other wildlife, dogs, and people. Actually, the "epidemic" was solely in the press; *Giardia* were first identified in the 18th century and are present in the public water system of many cities of the world and many towns in America—including some in the foothills of the Cascades. Long before the "outbreak" of "beaver fever" there was the well-known malady, the "Boy Scout trots." This is not to make light of the disease; though most humans feel no ill effects (but become carriers), others have serious symptoms which include devastating diarrhea, and the treatment is nearly as unpleasant. The reason giardiasis has become "epidemic" is that there are more people in the backcountry—more people drinking water contaminated by animals—more people contaminating the water.

Whenever in doubt, boil the water 10 minutes. Keep in mind that *Giardia* can survive in water at or near freezing for weeks or months—a snow pond is not necessarily safe. Boiling is 100 percent effective against not only *Giardia* but also the myriad other filthy little blighters that may upset your digestion or—as with some forms of hepatitis—destroy your liver.

If you cannot boil, use one of the several *iodine* treatments (chlorine compounds have been found untrustworthy in wildland circumstances), such as Potable Aqua or the more complicated method that employs iodine crystals. Pontificating by pseudo-experts to the contrary, medical scientists testify that iodine treatments pose no threat to the health.

Be very wary of the filters sold in backpacking shops. One or two have been tested and found fairly reliable (not against hepatitis, however), and new products are coming on the market, but most filters presently available are useless or next to it.

Cross-country Hiking

Much of the Park backcountry is trailless, kept that way to preserve some areas in as natural a condition as possible. When following a maintained trail a hiker must stick to the path to avoid extending the area of boot damage, which is particularly serious in fragile alpine plant communities. He should walk on the trail, not beside it. He should not cut switchbacks. When the tread is snow-covered, he should walk on the snow rather than detouring through meadows.

Cross-country camping is allowed for parties which have obtained the necessary permits, which are issued for groups only of five or fewer members. However, cross-country hikers must take special care not to leave marks of their passing. Following are some of the techniques by which one can minimize impact:

Do not hike where others have. Spread out instead of going single-file. Too many boots crushing plants cause erosion and new trails.

Follow the gentlest slope when ascending or descending to keep boots from digging in, crushing plants and disturbing the soil. Where possible hike on rock or snow or through forest.

Camp in timber or rocky areas rather than on meadows. Do not camp where others have. Remove every vestige of your stay.

Enjoy wildlife from a distance, forgoing close-up photos, in order not to cause animals and birds to alter their natural habits.

Do not mark your way with cairns, flags, or other markers which encourage others to follow your footsteps. Navigate with map and compass.

Make your toilet away from watercourses. Dig a small hole about 3–6 inches deep in organic material (the biological disposer level) and replace soil when finished. Use snow, dead vegetation, or biodegradable paper. Better, carry doubled, double-strength plastic bags, and pack it out.

Use tents and clothing that blend into the landscape. Avoid loud noises. Let others enjoy the solitude unaware of your presence.

Litter and Garbage

Ours is a throwaway civilization, but it is bad wildland manners to leave litter for someone else to worry about, especially in a National Park. The rule among thoughtful hikers is: **If you can carry it in full, you can carry it out empty.**

Other actions should be self-evident matters of ecological courtesy:

On a day hike, take back to the road (and garbage can) every last orange peel and gum-wrapper.

On an overnight hike, carry back everything, including metal, plastic, glass, and paper.

Don't bury garbage. If fresh, animals will dig it up and scatter the remnants. The Park is not large enough to hide underground all the cans and bottles and debris. Tin cans may take more than 80 years to disappear completely; aluminum and glass last for centuries. Further, digging pits to bury junk disturbs the ground cover, and iron often leaches from buried cans and "rusts" springs and creeks.

Don't leave leftover food for the next travelers; they will have their own food and won't be tempted by contributions spoiled by time or chewed by animals.

Especially don't cache plastic tarps. Weathering quickly ruins the fabric, little creatures nibble, and the result is a useless, miserable mess.

Bears

If every hiker were to scrupulously avoid advertising himself as proprietor of a traveling supermarket, the "bear problem" would completely disappear in a very few years, the animals quickly reverting to their natural foods. This must become every hiker's goal.

The problem cannot be solved by merely hanging food bags from trees. Bears which develop a dependence on man's bounty quickly learn to climb the tree and make a flying leap for the bag. It is necessary for all—

Black bear near Paradise Ranger Station

not just some—hikers to conspire to keep from bears the secret that back-packers carry eatables. This may be done by:

Never leaving a scrap of garbage, not even cracker crumbs "for the chipmunks." Never tossing bacon grease or fish guts or the like in the bushes. **Pack it out.**

If allowed sufficient time, a hungry bear will gain access to an un-tended food cache. Always keep food in tight containers to prevent aromas from spreading in the breeze. Always keep these containers in a tough food bag in a closed pack near the party. Hanging food between trees is effective, but Park personnel are concerned about damage done to frequently used trees. Although difficult to find in the lower 49 states, special odor-proof bags used by hikers in Alaska are recommended by the Park Supervisor.

Theft

Twenty years ago theft from a car left at a forest or National Park trailhead was rare. Not now. Equipment has become so fancy and ex-pensive, so much worth stealing, and hikers so numerous, their throngs creating large assemblages of valuables, that theft is a growing problem. Not even wilderness camps are entirely safe; a single raider hitting an unguarded camp may easily carry off several sleeping bags, a couple of tents, and assorted stoves, down booties, and freeze-dried strawberries—maybe $1000 worth of gear in one load! However, the professionals who do most of the stealing mainly concentrate on cars. Authorities are con-cerned but can't post guards at every trailhead.

National Park rangers have the following recommendations:

First and foremost, don't make crime profitable for the pros. If they break into a hundred cars and get nothing but moldy boots and tattered T-shirts, they'll give up. The best bet is to arrive in a beat-up 1960 car with doors and windows that don't close and leave in it nothing of value. If you insist on driving a nice new car, at least don't have mag wheels, tape deck, and radio, and keep it empty of gear. Don't think locks help—pros can open your car door and trunk as fast with a picklock as you can with your key. Don't imagine you can hide anything from them—they know all the hiding spots. If the hike is part of an extended car trip, ar-range to store your extra equipment at a nearby motel.

Be suspicious of anyone loitering around a trailhead. One of the tricks of the trade is to sit there with a pack as if waiting for a ride, watching new arrivals unpack—and hide their valuables—and maybe even strik-ing up a conversation to determine how long the marks will be away.

The ultimate solution, of course, is for hikers to become as poor as they were in the olden days. No criminal would consider trailheads profitable if the loot consisted solely of shabby khaki war surplus.

Climbing Mount Rainier

The summit of Mount Rainier has an irresistible attraction, and each year about 8500 people start for the summit; some 4000 succeed. There are only three regulations:

1. Registration is required.

Climbing on the Cowlitz Glacier

2. Those under 18 years of age must have written permission of a parent or guardian.

3. The climbing party must be made up of two or more people. (Solo climbs are allowed only with written permission of the Park superintendent.)

The popular climbing season is from the second weekend in May through the second weekend in September.

Before trying for the summit, check with your physician, then get into top condition by taking strenuous hikes every weekend and jogging several miles each day. Take every opportunity to walk or run instead of riding.

There are two ways to prepare for a climb. The best is to enroll in a climbing school offered by a mountaineering club, master the fundamentals of the sport on lesser peaks, and come to Mount Rainier fully qualified to tackle it.

A second way is to join a professionally guided party at Paradise. The guide service is used by novices and good climbers short of knowledge of glacier travel and crevasse rescue. The inexperienced climber must first spend a day at the guide-operated school learning crevasse rescue and use of ice ax and rope. Guides furnish their clients the necessary equipment. Full information can be obtained by writing the Superintendent, Mount Rainier National Park, Ashford, Washington 98304. Phone (206) 569-2211.

Unguided parties must register and obtain a backcountry use permit at Park headquarters or any ranger station. Permits are available during the hours the ranger stations are open; these hours vary.

The following personal equipment is needed: climbing boots, full-frame steel crampons (that fit), ice ax, three prusik slings, adequate inner and outer clothing, mittens, sunglasses or goggles, sun cream, first aid kit, food, and sleeping bag. The following party equipment is required: climbing rope equal to or better than ⅜-inch synthetic fiber, a minimum of one 120-foot rope for each three persons, topographic map, compass, and flashlights or headlights. The following equipment is recommended: stove, matches, extra food and clothing, wands, water bottle, carabiners, hard hats, pulleys, and tarp or tent. Most of these items can be rented or purchased from the guide service at Paradise. At the time of check-in, rangers will provide information on current route conditions.

The two most popular routes to the summit are by way of Camp Muir-Ingraham Glacier and Camp Schurman-Emmons Glacier. Both require two or more days.

The first day on the Muir-Ingraham route is spent checking out and hiking from Paradise to Camp Muir (Hike 45). The climb begins between 1 and 3 the following morning, to take advantage of firm snow that turns to mush under the afternoon sun. The route crosses the Cowlitz Glacier and climbs beside the Ingraham Glacier to the top, but the way changes from week to week as crevasses open and ice bridges break. Allow 6 to 8 hours from Camp Muir to the summit, and 2 to 3 hours to descend. There is a limit on the number of people camping in a particular location. The limits include 110 private individuals at Camp Muir plus RMI clients, 36 individuals at Ingraham Flats, 36 individuals on the Muir Snowfield.

Air view of the crater on Columbia Crest, Liberty Cap to the right. Notice the difficulty of crossing the top bergschrund.

These restrictions control numbers of climbers on a route because most people need to camp somewhere. There is no specific limit on the number of climbers using a given route at any one time.

The Schurman—Emmons route is generally easier. However, the starting point is much lower and the hiking distance considerably longer. For this reason many prefer to spend 2½ days. From the White River Campground, follow the trail to Glacier Basin (Hike 22) and perhaps the first night's camp. Leave trail and climb Interglacier to Steamboat Prow and high camp near Schurman Hut (an emergency cabin). The departure time next morning is between midnight and 4. The route varies considerably during the summer but for much of the ascent follows "The Corridor," a relatively smooth snow ridge dividing the Emmons and Winthrop glaciers. The biggest problem usually is finding a route from the top of The Corridor through the breakups and around or over the big bergschrund near the top. Some years there isn't any easy way.

This Land Is Your Land

Some of the above paragraphs may strike a hiker raised in the frontier tradition as being too heavy on "don'ts." However, neither The Mountaineers nor the National Park Service seeks to restrict freedom of enjoyment. Rather, the intent is to suggest how one may enjoy the Park without destroying the pleasure of others who will follow the same trails tomorrow, next summer, and in years to come.

Mount Rainier National Park is the property of every American. For each of us and all of us, it is home, if we make it so, and treat it so.

Safety Considerations

The reason the Ten Essentials are advised is that hiking in the backcountry entails unavoidable risk which every hiker assumes and must be aware of and respect. The fact that a trail is described in this book is not a representation that it will be safe for you. Trails vary greatly in difficulty and in the degree of conditioning and agility needed to enjoy them safely. On some hikes routes may have changed or conditions deteriorated since the descriptions were written. Also, trail conditions can change even from day to day, owing to weather and other factors. A trail that is safe on a dry day or for a highly conditioned, agile, properly equipped hiker may be completely unsafe for someone else or unsafe under adverse weather conditions.

You can minimize your risks on the trail by being knowledgeable, prepared, and alert. There is not space in this book for a general treatise on safety in the mountains, but there are a number of good books and public courses on the subject, and you should take advantage of them to increase your knowledge. Just as important, you should always be aware of your own limitations and of conditions existing when and where you are hiking. If conditions are dangerous, or if you are not prepared to deal with them safely, choose a different hike! It's better to have a wasted drive than to be the subject of a mountain rescue.

These warnings are not intended to scare you off the trails. Hundreds of thousands of people have safe and enjoyable hikes every year. However, one element of the beauty, freedom, and excitement of the wilderness is the presence of risks that do not confront us at home. When you hike you assume those risks. They can be met safely, but only if you exercise your own independent judgment and common sense.

EXPLANATION OF SYMBOLS

Easy strolls. No special clothing or equipment required. Hikes which can be accomplished by nearly everybody in a day or less.

Hikes requiring at least a minimum of equipment—lug-soled boots, sturdy clothing, rucksack with the Ten Essentials. (See page 10.)

Hikes especially suited for overnight trips. Although most of the hikes in this book can be completed round trip in a day by a strong hiker carrying only a light rucksack, these trips are recommended for overnight outings.

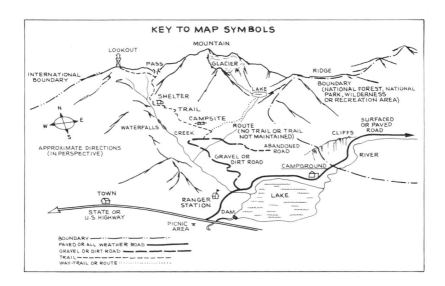

Avalanche lilies

False Solomon's seal

Elephant head, one of the figwort family

(opposite) Beargrass

Raccoons at Longmire

Cascades golden-mantled ground squirrel

Clark's nutcracker

1 EAGLE PEAK SADDLE

Round trip 7 miles (11 km)
Hiking time 5 hours
High point 5650 feet

Elevation gain 2955 feet
Snowfree July to October

A forest hike to a great view of Mount Rainier from a high saddle on the west end of the Tatoosh Range.

Drive from National Park Inn at Longmire past the ranger station and residences, cross the suspension bridge over the Nisqually River, and park in front of the community house, elevation 2780 feet. Walk back up the road toward the bridge. Sometimes the road is closed, in which case park in the Longmire parking area. Cross the bridge and continue 200 feet to trailhead on the left.

Most of the hike lies in virgin forest on a wide, smooth path with an easy grade. The first mile is an aisle through a dense undercover of salal. Around 2 miles is a small stream, the last water. At about 3¼ miles, good trail ends below a high-angle meadow, which in late June explodes with flowers, the Tatoosh Range adding an inspiring backdrop for the fields of bear grass. A final steep and rocky ½ mile climbs to the 5700-foot saddle, where all semblance of trail disappears.

Walk a short way to the right for the best view of Mount Rainier. East is the Tatoosh Range. West and down is Longmire. South rise Adams and St. Helens, beyond miles and miles of private tree farms and the Gifford Pinchot National Forest. Eagle Peak is very close to the Park boundary, providing a good opportunity to see the difference between multiple-use lands and a "museum of primitive America."

The saddle is the essential turnaround for hikers; the final 300 feet to

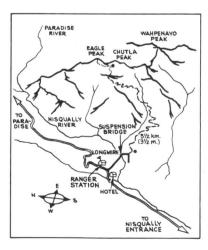

Gray jay

Mount Rainier from Eagle Peak saddle

the summit of Eagle Peak are strictly for experienced climbers. They consider the summit ascent easy enough; the rock is solid and the ledge wide. However, the danger of a fall is great. In any event, the view from the saddle is just as good as that from the top.

$\overline{\underline{2}}$ TRAIL OF THE SHADOWS

Loop trip ¾ mile (1 km)
Hiking time 30 minutes
Snowfree ⅔ of the year

The Trail of the Shadows is a self-guiding nature walk that winds past mineral springs and a cabin built in 1888 and through a lovely cool forest.

Drive from the Nisqually Entrance 6 miles to Longmire. Trail begins directly across the highway from the hotel, elevation 2750 feet. Outstanding trail features are numbered and keyed to a booklet, copies of which may be picked up at the trailhead. To follow the booklet, go counterclockwise on the loop.

The center of the loop is mostly marshy meadow with active beaver dams and numerous mineral springs, some tepid; the trail passes near two of the springs. James Longmire, on a trip to Paradise, discovered the springs, which were considerably warmer then. In 1884 he staked a mineral claim and established a hotel. The existing cabin was built by his son in 1888 on a homestead claim.

The trail continues past the cabin into dense forest. Three-fourths of the way around is the junction with the trail over Rampart Ridge (Hike 3).

Lovely in all seasons, in October the trail gives its final color show before the snows, a display of strikingly beautiful—but deadly—gold-and-orange amanita mushrooms. Remember: for all to enjoy, nothing should be removed.

Homestead cabin on Trail of the Shadows

Twin Firs Loop Trail:

A grove of large trees and nurse logs, a fine example of a climax forest, on a ½-mile loop. Drive exactly 0.9 mile toward Longmire from the Kautz Creek bridge or 2.1 miles from Longmire toward the Nisqually Entrance to a small paved parking area and interpretative sign on the north side of the road.

The trail starts behind the twin firs, parallels the road a few feet, climbs uphill, crossing several small streams, and then descends and ends within a few feet of the starting point. Fallen timber makes the trail difficult to follow.

Cougar Rock to Longmire:

From the entrance to Cougar Rock Campground, cross the highway and walk down the shoulder to the first curve to locate the trail. The way passes through a pleasant forest between the highway and the Nisqually River, sometimes in sight of the stream. One-way distance 2 miles, all downhill.

Carter Falls:

A mile-long walk to Carter Falls on a surviving segment of the 1895 trail to Paradise Valley.

Drive toward Paradise to the last bend before Cougar Rock Campground and park on the wide shoulder overlooking the river. Cross the Nisqually River on a footbridge. The way then follows an old service road to the site of a powerhouse that occasionally supplied electricity to the Park from 1924 until the late 1960s. It was removed in 1986.

The route becomes true trail. Note the old mileage markers on trees, starting with 1.8 (miles from Longmire); these were used throughout the Park in the 1930s. Just above the trail is a large wooden pipeline that carried water, under pressure, to the powerhouse. At ¾ mile note a large cedar tree with numerous woodpecker holes. It is suspected that the charred wood dates from the occasion when Longmire burned out a wasp nest that harassed his horse train. In a long mile, after a 500-foot climb, reach Carter Falls.

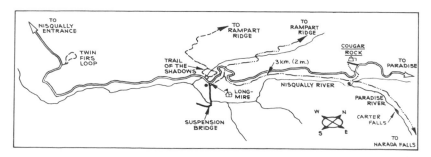

Tumtum Peak from Rampart Ridge trail

3 RAMPART RIDGE

Loop trip 4.5 miles (7¼ km)
Hiking time 2½ hours
High point 4080 feet

Elevation gain 1800 feet
Snowfree mid-June to October

A loop trip through fine forests, climbing to a cliff-edge panorama of the Nisqually River valley. The trail is in excellent condition, but carry water. There is none on the way.

Drive to Longmire, where the hike begins and ends. It doesn't really matter which direction is taken, but by going clockwise one has glimpses of The Mountain while walking along the ridge.

Find the Trail of the Shadows nature walk directly across the road from the National Park Inn, elevation 2750 feet. Take the **left** (reverse) segment of the loop 800 feet, to a junction with the Rampart Ridge trail.

The wide path ascends through woods 2 miles, in a series of long switchbacks, to the ridge crest. The last switchback gives an interesting view of Tumtum Peak to the west. Then comes a cliff-top overlook of Longmire and the entire Nisqually River valley, all the way up to the buildings at Paradise.

Shortly beyond, the trail levels into a flat mile along the ridge. At the junction with the Wonderland Trail, go right. In a bit is another junction, this time with a trail to Van Trump Park; again go right, dropping into the valley. Just before reaching Longmire the trail crosses the road; pick it up again on the far side and return to the parking lot.

Those who want views will find excellent vistas on the ridge.

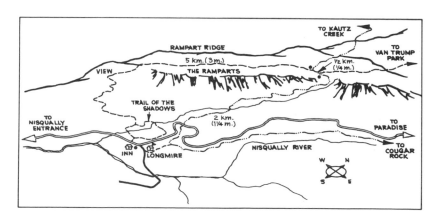

4 KAUTZ CREEK

Round trip 11 miles (17½ km)
Hiking time 6 hours
High point 5600 feet

Elevation gain 2300 feet in, 200
feet out
Snowfree mid-July to mid-
October

A trail with a long history—the earliest route to Indian Henry's Hunting Ground—begins in the Kautz Creek flood area and passes through forest to the high meadow country.

Hikers on their first trip to Indian Henry's will want to save time and energy for explorations when they get there, and thus should take the shorter route up Tahoma Creek, if it ever reopens (see Hike 5). However, though 2 miles longer, the Kautz Creek trail is the more interesting, giving an unusual perspective of The Mountain. If doing the hike early in the summer, make sure before starting that the footbridge is in place over the creek; high water frequently washes it away.

Drive from the Nisqually Entrance 3 miles toward Longmire and park near the nature exhibit at the Kautz Creek bridge, elevation 2378 feet. The trail starts on the opposite side of the highway.

The trail winds a short and easy way along the smooth top of the Kautz Mudflow, crosses Kautz Creek, and then enters virgin forest. The next stretch is a gentle climb, followed by a steep series of switchbacks pulling out of the valley.

In about 4 miles the trail moderates a bit and enters meadows with views south and west. Farther along, Point Success, the second-highest of Mount Rainier's three summits, can be seen poking over the ridge ahead. Early in the season there is some very muddy tread on a steep hillside. Finally the grade levels, and the last ¾ mile traverses around the flank of Mt. Ararat and drops down to Indian Henry's. (Mt. Ararat

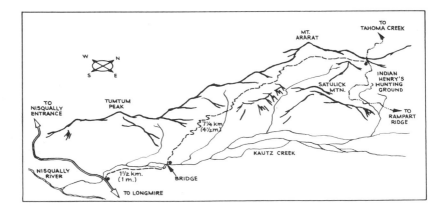

was named by Ben Longmire, who claimed to have found on this peak
some petrified planks and a petrified stump with what appeared to be an
old cable scar around it. Thus, this must have been where Noah's ark
first touched land.)

5 INDIAN HENRY'S HUNTING GROUND

Round trip from Kautz Creek
11 miles (17½ km)
Hiking time 6 hours
High point 5600 feet

Elevation gain 2300 feet in,
200 feet out
Snowfree mid-July to mid-
October

One of the Park's loveliest alpine meadows; in season, a blaze of flowers. A highlight is the view of Mount Rainier from Mirror Lake, a view made famous on a 1934 postage stamp. The lake is reached from a ¾-mile spur trail that starts in the big meadow below the patrol cabin. The closest backcountry campsite is on Wonderland Trail 1 mile east toward Longmire and 300 feet lower.

The popular Tahoma Creek trail to Indian Henry's is presently impassable, obliterated in the same flood that closed the West Side Road, as described below. For now, the only practical approach is by way of the Kautz Creek trail (Hike 4).

The West Side Road

A section of the West Side Road has been obliterated by recurring flash floods originating under the Kautz Glacier high on Mount Ranier. These are miniature kin to the Ice Age floods that carved the Grand Coulee region of Eastern Washington. Time after time the continental ice sheet dammed the Columbia River, and time after time the dam broke and water of the huge lake came a-whooshing oceanward, resulting in coulees of the "Channeled Scabland." On a much smaller scale, since 1986 the Kautz Glacier has been damming its creek, and at unpredictable times the ice has given way and loosed floods down the valley, uprooting trees, rolling house-sized boulders, and washing out a section of the West Side Road—which is repaired, then washed out again and again. The flash floods come without warning; on occasion tourists have

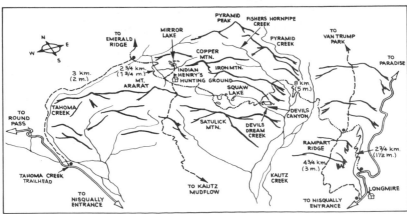

Mirror Lake and Mount Rainier taken from the same place as Asahel Curtis's famous picture used on a 1934 postage stamp

nearly had encounters of the Third Kind. The Mountain thus has been conceded victory in its argument with the road, which will remain closed until the glacier settles down.

A bypass has been provided around the washout for hikers and bicyclists to reach trailheads, but note: *Bicycles are not allowed on trails, only on the roadway.*

Losing the popular day hikes to Gobblers Knob, Emerald Ridge, and Klapatche Park is regretted. However, the exciting presence of a Living Mountain more than compensates. Drive the West Side Road to the washout. Gape at what havoc Nature has wrought. St. Helens isn't the only big show in these parts.

6 GOBBLERS KNOB

To Lake George:
    Round trip 10 miles (16 km)
    Hiking time 6 hours
    High point 1900 feet
    Elevation gain 700 feet
    Snowfree June through
    October

To Gobblers Knob:
    Round trip 13 miles (21 km)
     from trailhead
    Hiking time 8 hours
    High point 5488 feet
    Elevation gain 3000 feet
    Snowfree July to mid-October

A wide, well-beaten path to a mountain lake tucked away in forest and to a fire lookout with a grand view of Tahoma Glacier and Sunset Amphitheater.

From the Nisqually Entrance, drive 1 mile and go right 3 miles on the West Side Road to the washout, elevation 2500 feet. On foot, walk the road 4 miles to Round Pass, elevation 3900 feet. Trail is on the left side of the road.

The smooth trail, probably the most popular on the west side of the mountain, gains elevation steadily but easily, reaching Lake George in a bit less than 1 mile. The lake, almost ½ mile long, is a popular campsite both for fishermen and beginning hikers on their first backpack. There is a shelter—usually full. A way trail goes around the right-hand shore, to views of Mount Rainier.

The trail climbs a somewhat steeper but still quite gentle 1½ miles from the lake to Gobblers Knob, the most northerly bump on the long ridge of Mt. Wow. A short distance below the top, a 1½-mile side-trail drops to Goat Lake, outside the Park in the Glacier View Wilderness;

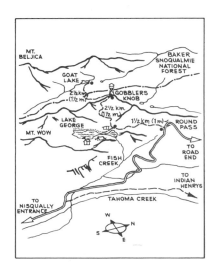

Alpine Fir tree on side of Gobbler's Knob

Mount Rainier from Gobblers Knob

camping at Goat Lake is more private than at Lake George. Beyond the junction the way emerges from forest to the odd and striking cliffs of the Knob, a rock garden of juniper, red heather, phlox, and other flowers in season.

The horizon from the lookout cabin is all Mount Rainier on one side—but on others, St. Helens, Adams, Hood, and the Olympic Mountains. A substantial reward for a leisurely afternoon.

7 EMERALD RIDGE

Round trip 16 miles (26 km)
Hiking time 10 hours
High point 5600 feet

Elevation gain 3400 feet
Snowfree July to mid-October

Take a little-used access to the Wonderland Trail and then climb beside the Tahoma Glacier to an emerald-green ridge with a close-up look at living ice and an unusual view of The Mountain.

From the Nisqually Entrance, drive 1 mile and go right 3 miles on the West Side Road to the washout, elevation 2500 feet. On foot, travel 4.5 miles, crossing over Round Pass to the trailhead shortly before crossing the bridge over the very muddy South Fork Puyallup River, elevation 3550 feet.

The trail passes through a deep forest, including giant cedars. In 1½ miles look for tall colonnades of columnar andesite, one of the finest examples in the Park. The columns (usually hexagonal) were formed when hot lava flowed into the valley; the pattern developed as a result of shrinkage during cooling. Shortly beyond are a backcountry campsite and a junction with the Wonderland Trail. The left fork crosses the river and ascends to St. Andrews Park and Klapatche Park (Hike 8).

The right fork climbs to the ridge in about 2 miles, following old moraines and riverbeds full of cobblestones, becoming steeper, but still easy enough going. Note the variety of evergreen and deciduous trees reforesting the morainal debris. As elevation is gained the Tahoma Glacier comes in sight, its flow split by Emerald Ridge into two tongues, the northeast lobe providing the source of the South Fork Puyallup River.

The ridge top is a small, open, very green meadow, though with few flowers. Watch for goats. The "prow" of the ridge offers a splendid view

The Colonnades

Emerald Ridge and Glacier Island

up the glacier to Tokaloo Rock and the Puyallup Cleaver. To the right is the prominent cliff of Glacier Island, which until 40 years ago was completely surrounded by ice; now only barren moraines are left at its base.

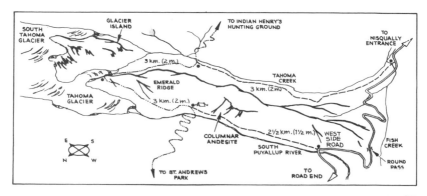

8

KLAPATCHE PARK

Round trip to Klapatche 21 miles   **Elevation gain 3000 feet**
   (35 km)   **Snowfree mid-July to mid-**
Hiking time 2 days   **October**
High point 5500 feet

An all-time favorite camp near a subalpine pond, a water-mirror ringed by soft and fragile meadows. Magnificent view of Sunset Amphitheater and dramatic sunsets. Klapatche can be a good day trip, an overnight trip, or a loop trip.

From the Nisqually Entrance, drive 1 mile and go right 3 miles on the West Side Road to the washout, elevation 2500 feet. On foot, travel 8 miles climbing over Round Pass, lose 500 feet, then regain 300 feet to St. Andrews Creek trail, elevation 3700 feet. The wide, smooth way climbs steadily through forest to the ridge crest, which it then follows for 2½ miles, with a few views, to a surprisingly abrupt opening into meadows at Aurora Lake.

Sometimes dry in late August, before then the lakelet reflects parkland trees, towering clouds—and Mount Rainier. A few campsites are tucked in the trees on the west shore.

The side-trip to St. Andrews Park is mandatory. Follow the Wonderland Trail uphill ¾ mile through flower gardens, past a grand overlook of the mountain, to 6000-foot St. Andrews Lake. About the time Aurora Lake is drying up, this one is just melting out.

For an interesting loop trip adding 3 miles and 1500 feet elevation gain to the trip, continue walking the West Side Road another mile to Klapatche Point, then downhil 2¾ miles to campsites near the North Puyallup River bridge. Don't cross the bridge, but go right on the Wonderland Trail, climbing 1500 feet in 2¾ miles to Klapatche Park. The loop route can be done either way, but is recommended clockwise because facing Mount Rainier breaks the monotony while walking the road.

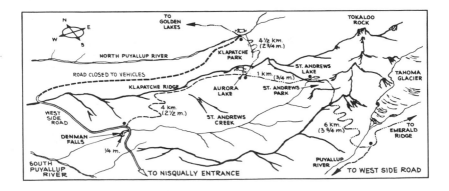

Aurora Lake and Mount Rainier from Klapatche Park

On the return trip, if time permits, be sure to take the 20-minute side-trip from the parking lot down the cool forest path ¼ mile to Denman Falls.

9

SUNSET PARK AND GOLDEN LAKES

Round trip 16 miles (25 km)
Hiking time 10 hours
High point 5500 feet

Elevation gain 2400 feet in, 1100
feet out
Snowfree July to mid-October

The West Side Road most closely approaches Sunset Park, but has such problems (specifically, a gate kept locked due to certain environmental hazards associated with active volcanoes) that the quickest route is from the road to Mowich Lake.

From the Mowich Entrance, drive ½ mile to the Paul Peak picnic area, elevation 3700 feet. The trail leaves the right side of the picnic area, descends gradually, rounds Paul Peak, and at 3½ miles joins the Wonderland Trail. Take the right fork, crossing a log bridge to the Mowich River backcountry campsite; several shelters are spotted between the North and South Mowich Rivers, 2600 feet. From here the trail heads upward in a series of switchbacks, climbing 2400 feet in the next 4 miles to Golden Lakes, 5000 feet.

Sidetrails lead to the lakes. For views continue on the Wonderland Trail another 1 mile and turn left at an unsigned junction. The easy climb through open meadows seems to be intent on burrowing into The Mountain but in fact ends at Lookout Point, site of the former Sunset Lookout. Look up to Sunset Amphitheater and ice cliffs on Ptarmigan Ridge and down to the Golden Lakes, and out to the sunset which colors them, and afterwards to the novas of Puget Sound cities.

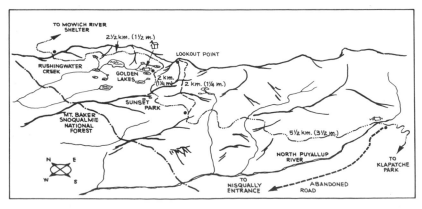

Mount Rainier from trail to Golden Lakes

10 PAUL PEAK TRAIL

Round trip (to Mowich River
Shelter) 7½ miles (12 km)
Hiking time 3 hours
High point 4200 feet

Elevation gain 800 feet in, 1900
feet out
Snowfree April or May through
October

A hike through deep timber, ideal for spring and autumn hiking when higher trails are under snow. Short on vistas but long on virgin forest, ethereal in fall mists. Keep an eye out for mushrooms, both the safely edibles and the eyes-only.

Drive the Mowich Entrance road to the Paul Peak picnic area ½ mile inside the Park boundary, elevation 3700 feet. The trail leaves the right side of the picnic area, descends gradually, rounds Paul Peak, and at 3½ miles joins the Wonderland Trail. Take the right fork, crossing a log bridge to the Mowich River backcountry campsite where several shelters are spotted between the North and South Mowich Rivers. This side of the mountain has so few visitors the shelters are often vacant.

During summer months when high trails are snowfree, a loop trip can be made by way of Mowich Lake. Recross the North Mowich River and follow the Wonderland Trail, which in 2 miles switchbacks, climbing 2000 feet up from the river, then levels out to a gently-climbing mile along Crater Creek to Mowich Lake and the road-end.

Rather than walk all the way back on the road, at .2 mile down the road from the lake find the unmaintained Grindstone Trail and use it to shortcut the long switchbacks required by passenger cars. The trail was built by Bailey Willis in 1884 and provided the first "tourist" access to Rainier's high meadowlands. Follow it ¾ mile and then rejoin the road to the starting point for a total round-trip hike of 12 miles.

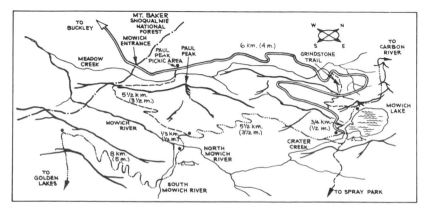

Twinflower growing near the Mowich River trail

11 TOLMIE PEAK

Round trip 6½ miles (10½ km)
Hiking time 3 hours
High point 5939 feet

Elevation gain 1200 feet in, 200
feet out
Snowfree mid-July through
September

A view supreme and a serene alpine lake. This is the peak long thought to have been climbed in 1833 by Dr. Tolmie, first European to visit what is now the Park. (Recent research indicates Tolmie actually climbed Hessong Rock, closer to the mountain.)

Drive via Buckley and Wilkeson to the Mowich Entrance and continue to road-end at Mowich Lake, elevation 5000 feet. The road is generally rough, but passable at slow speeds. Before reaching the Park one can enjoy (if that is the word) an enormous panorama of clearcut logging from the valleys up onto the slopes of The Mountain itself.

Find the Wonderland Trail on the left side of the road just on arriving at the lake. The path skirts the forested shores on a fairly level grade, rising and falling a bit. At 1¼ miles is Ipsut Pass, where the Wonderland Trail descends right 4 miles to the Carbon River (Hike 15). Take the left fork another 1 mile to Eunice Lake, first dropping 100 feet, then in the final ½ mile turning steeply up.

Eunice Lake, at an elevation of 5355 feet, is one of the prettiest lakes in the Park. Rising above is Tolmie Peak, the lookout cabin plainly visible. Follow the trail around the left shore and see Mount Rainier across the foreground of wind-rippling, sun-sparkling water.

The meadows around the lake are extremely fragile and should not be compelled to endure the punishment of feet. Though not the vast flower fields of Spray Park or Paradise, they display almost all the same species.

The trip is incomplete without climbing the steep but short 1 mile to the lookout. South is Mt. St. Helens, west the Olympics, and north Mt.

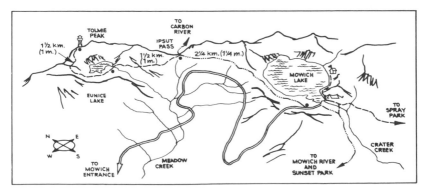

Eunice Lake and Mount Rainier from trail to Tolmie Peak

Baker. Directly below on one side is Green Lake (Hike 14), and on the other Eunice Lake, and off where the hike began, Mowich Lake. North is the immense logging scar on Cayada Creek. Southeast, of course, is The Mountain.

12 SPRAY PARK

Round trip (to the broad meadow under Mt. Pleasant) about 6 miles (9½ km)
Hiking time 3 hours
High point 5800 feet

Elevation gain 2200 feet in, 300 feet out
Snowfree mid-July through October

Every Rainier hiker has his favorite, but many argue this is the supreme flower garden in the Park. Pond-sprinkled meadows, easy-roaming ridges, endless and delightful nooks and crannies. In the past as many as 185 campers were counted at Spray Park, with another 200 day hikers. To let the meadows recover from years of such impact, camping is now prohibited. However, camping is allowed at Mowich Lake and Eagle Roost Camp near Spray Falls.

Drive via Buckley and Wilkeson to the Mowich Entrance and continue to the road-end at Mowich Lake, elevation 4929 feet.

Find the Wonderland Trail near the lake outlet and descend ¼ mile to a split. The Wonderland goes right; go left on the Spray Park trail, up a little, down a little, through subalpine forest, around the side of Fay Peak and Hessong Rock. At 1½ miles is Eagle Cliff, a fine spot to sit for a long look at The Mountain, especially the Mowich Glacier. Past Eagle's Roost backcountry campsite, a side-trail crosses a footlog and goes ¼ mile to Spray Falls, a wide splash of water; only a fraction of the falls can be seen—the main part is uphill, out of sight—but what can be seen is beautiful enough.

From the falls the trail switchbacks steeply up some 600 feet in ½ mile to the lowermost meadows of Spray Park. Day hikers often have lunch here and turn around, well satisfied with the flowers and with the glaciers beyond 7800-foot Echo Rock and 8300-foot Observation Rock. However, the first really broad meadow, under Mt. Pleasant, is another

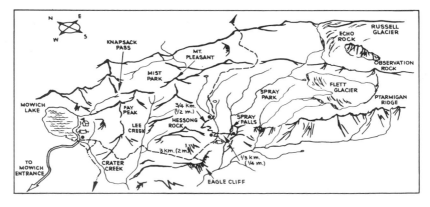

Mount Rainier and avalanche lilies in Spray Park

few minutes, and the farther one goes, the better the views. Continue on the trail to the 6400-foot ridge above Seattle Park (Hike 16); on a clear day the view extends all the way beyond lower buttresses of Mount Rainier to the North Cascades.

June Creek nature trail

MOWICH LAKE AND CARBON RIVER

13 CARBON RIVER TRAILS

The Olympic rain forest—that's what one is reminded of when walking in the cool, damp growth of the Carbon River valley, seeing the moss-draped trees, the soft carpet of moss on the ground, the classic examples of nurse logs, and all the thriving life in the green-gloomy understory.

Drive via Buckley and Wilkeson to the Carbon River Entrance, elevation 1750 feet. No trail runs the length of the forest but several short spurs offer easy samples.

Rain Forest Loop Nature Trail:

This is one of the few known inland examples of temperate rain forest, which usually occurs near the ocean coast.

On the right side of the road at the Park entrance, find the self-

48

guiding nature trail. The ½-mile loop leads partly through a marsh and partly through trees, with numbered steps discussing the rain-forest environment.

Chenuis Falls:

Drive about 3½ miles from the Park entrance to parking space and sign on the left. The trail crosses the Carbon River on a bridge and winds through forest a short bit to the falls, which cascade down a series of rock slabs. The bridge washes out almost every spring and isn't replaced until summer when the water recedes.

Ipsut Falls Trail:

An easy hike to a waterfall. From the trailhead at Ipsut Creek Campground, at the end of the Carbon River road, follow the Wonderland Trail south toward Mowich Lake ¼ mile. Just before the trail begins its uphill climb, take a side-trail right a few hundred feet to a view of the falls.

Carbon Glacier Viewpoint:

The most popular hike in the valley is to a viewpoint close to the snout of the Carbon Glacier. Most of the way is in forest with occasional views of Mount Rainier. The trail crosses the Carbon River on a swaying suspension bridge that scares off some hikers. If the lower bridge is in place, it provides an alternate route easier on the nerves.

From the Ipsut Creek Campground, hike upstream as described in Hike 17. At 2 miles, if that bridge is in place, go left for the alternate route. Otherwise continue a mile to the suspension bridge. A short distance beyond the crossing, turn uphill ¼ mile to the viewpoint. Don't be tempted to approach the glacier face; boulders frequently melt out and come bouncing down.

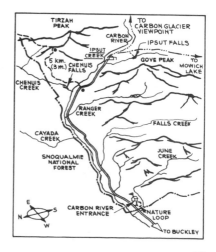

14 GREEN LAKE

Round trip 4 miles (6½ km)   **Elevation gain 1200 feet**
Hiking time 2 hours   **Snowfree May to November**
High point 3185 feet

In a National Park with many wonderful forest trails, this easy walk to a crystal-clear lake stands far above all the rest.

Drive to the Carbon River Entrance and 3 miles beyond to a small parking space at Ranger Creek crossing (a culvert), elevation 985 feet. Trail is on the right.

The beginning is a climb through a grove of giant trees, centuries old. During the first ½ mile the floor is rich in ferns and devil's club. One gnarled root system would serve as a proper throne for a forest prince. Above the path are numerous tree bridges—overpasses for squirrels, no doubt.

In 1 mile take a short-side-trip to Ranger Creek Falls. In 1½ miles the track levels and crosses the creek, and at 2 miles reaches the lake, deep in lush forest. (Because of extreme fire hazard in the deep forest duff, and the large number of visitors who easily could "love the lake to death," camping is not permitted.)

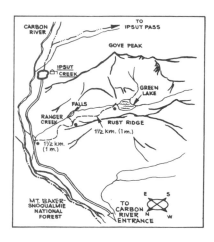

Ranger Creek trail

(opposite) Ranger Creek Falls

15 IPSUT CREEK

Round trip to Ipsut Pass 8 miles
(12¾ km)
Hiking time 4 hours
High point 5100 feet

Elevation gain 2800 feet
Snowfree June through October

A forested segment of the Wonderland Trail passing the world's largest known Alaska yellow-cedar. The woods walk as far as the big tree is pleasant in itself, particularly early in the season when the high country is buried in snow.

Drive to the Carbon River Entrance and continue to the road-end at Ipsut Creek Campground, elevation 2300 feet. The trail starts at the upper end of the camping area, follows the dirt road 300 feet, and turns right at a prominent sign. In a short distance climbing begins. The path is wide and mostly smooth. The trees are impressively tall, and the ground is carpeted with moss and flowers. The trail continues steadily upward, crossing numerous small streams. Ipsut Creek is a constant roar on the right.

In about 3 miles the way emerges from forest and crosses the creek, which though still noisy is now only a step wide. The specimen cedar is in a grove of subalpine trees just beyond the crossing. Actually, after the huge firs and hemlocks lower down, the largest Alaska yellow-cedar in the world doesn't look very impressive. However, many hundreds of years are required for that species to attain such size.

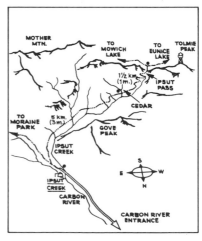

Largest known Alaska-cedar tree

Marmot near Ipsut Pass

The cedar is a good turnaround. Above here the way steepens to a series of short switchbacks up to 5100-foot Ipsut Pass. The most notable spot is a free shower from a waterfall under a tall cliff overhanging the trail.

This route is an alternate way to Tolmie Peak or Mowich Lake (Hike 11). From Ipsut Pass the lake is 1½ miles to the left and the peak 2 miles to the right.

16 SEATTLE PARK

Round trip to Seattle Park 12 miles (19 km)
Hiking time 7 hours
High point 5200 feet
Elevation gain 3000 feet
Snowfree mid-July to mid-October

Round trip to divide 16 miles (25 km)
Hiking time 10 hours
High point 6400 feet
Elevation gain 4200 feet
Snowfree mid-July to mid-October

A picturelike parkland of heather meadows interspersed with groves of subalpine trees. There are no campsites in Seattle Park, making it a long and very strenuous day hike from the road. However, camping is permitted at two closer spots.

Drive to the Carbon River Entrance and continue to road-end at Ipsut Creek Campground, elevation 2300 feet. Find the trail at the upper boundary of the camp. In ¼ mile go left on the Wonderland Trail.

Hike the easy grade partly on a long-abandoned road up the west side of the Carbon River, at 2 miles passing a trail that goes left across the river. Continue straight ahead to Carbon River Camp and Cataract Creek junction at 3 miles; go right.

Now come 3 miles of steady climbing, at 5 miles from the road passing the Cataract Valley camp to the first open meadow. Except for the last ½ mile the trail in the forest is nicely graded. At 6 miles from the road, on the edge of meadowland, is Marmot Creek, elevation 5200 feet, the usual turnaround. To fully appreciate the wide-open country of Seattle Park,

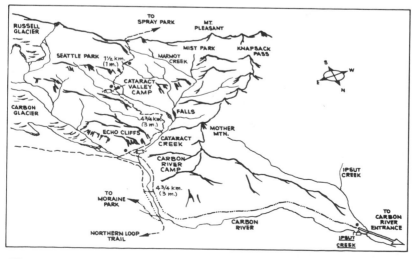

Mount Rainier from Seattle Park

continue at least another ½ mile, or better yet, 2 more miles, crossing permanent snowfields and topping the 6400-foot ridge above Spray Park (Hike 12).

17 MORAINE PARK— MYSTIC LAKE

Round trip to Mystic Lake 12 miles (19 km)
Hiking time 8 hours
High point 6004 feet

Elevation gain 3800 feet in, 400 feet out
Snowfree mid-July to October

A close look at the snout of the Carbon Glacier, lowest-elevation glacier in the old 48 states, flower meadows and high ridges for roaming, and a near view of enormous Willis Wall. If lucky, one may see avalanches seemingly float down the 3600-foot cliff.

Drive to the Carbon River Entrance and continue to road-end at Ipsut Creek Campground, elevation 2300 feet. Find the trail at the upper boundary of the camp. In ¼ mile go left on the Wonderland Trail.

The first 3 miles follow the valley above the river. Pass the Northern Loop junction at 2 miles and Carbon River Camp and Seattle Park junction at 3 miles; shortly beyond cross the Carbon River on a suspension bridge that makes some hikers turn pale and lose their knees. If the sway is too much for the nerves, go back to the Northern Loop Trail, cross the river on a log bridge, and hike up the far bank. A short distance beyond the suspension bridge is a junction; go right, uphill.

The trail steepens, gaining 1700 feet in 2 miles. In ⅓ mile pass a striking viewpoint of the Carbon Glacier snout. Though some other glaciers in the Park have receded almost a mile in the last 30 years, the Carbon has held its own. The next ½ mile is very rough, crossing rubbly, cliffy slopes hanging above the ice, but provides more views of the snout. In another mile is tumbling Dick Creek, a good rest stop; just beyond is Dick Creek Camp. The trail enters forest and smooths out, though it's still steep. The final stretch emerges in parkland and flattens.

Officially, Moraine Park is the rather small meadow between trail and glacier, but hikers generally refer to all the tree-and-flower slopes of lower Curtis Ridge as Moraine Park. The official Moraine Park is pretty

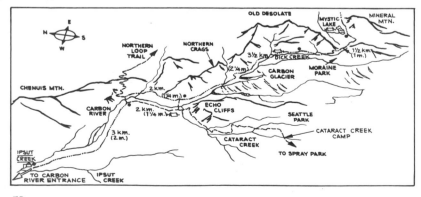

Mount Rainier reflected in alpine tarn at Moraine Park

enough, especially in flower season, but the best is farther ahead. Follow the trail up a steep mile to a 6004-foot saddle. A short drop leads to Mystic Lake and camps.

18 WINDY GAP— NATURAL BRIDGE

Round trip 14 miles (22 km)
Hiking time 9 hours
High point 5800 feet

Elevation gain 3500 feet in, 300
feet out
Snowfree mid-July to mid-
October

Hike a portion of the Northern Loop Trail to colorful cliffs, arctic-like tundra, and a natural bridge on Independence Ridge. Though the hike can be done in a long day, it is recommended as a backpack.

Drive to the Carbon River Entrance and continue to road-end at Ipsut Creek Campground, elevation 2300 feet. Find the Wonderland Trail at the upper boundary of the camp.

The first 2 miles follow the valley above the river. At a junction take the left fork across the Carbon River. The river often floods and frequently changes course, washing out the bridge; the exact point of crossing therefore varies. On the far side of the river is a split. The right fork heads upstream toward Moraine Park; turn left and follow the Northern Loop Trail.

The way goes down the valley a bit, then begins an unrelenting 3000-foot, 4-mile climb to Windy Gap. The first 3 miles are through forest on a smooth and soft path. At 3½ miles (5¼ miles from Ipsut Creek Campground) is Yellowstone Cliffs campsite. The final ¾ mile tends to be muddy and becomes an endless stairway, but the great meadows compensate for any muss. The trail rounds beneath Tyee Peak and the Yel-

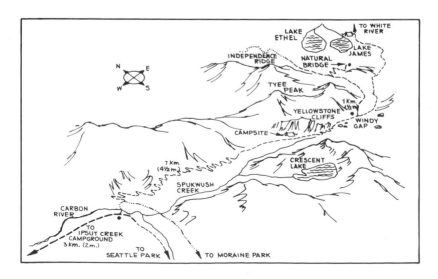

Natural Bridge

lowstone Cliffs and passes three shallow lakes before coming to 5800-foot Windy Gap, 6 miles from the road-end.

Continue over the pass a short distance to a fork. The Northern Loop Trail descends 2 miles to campsites at Lake James; go left, contouring ½ mile across the open slopes of Independence Ridge, in views to Fremont Lookout and Grand Park. Then switchback downhill, losing 200 feet, to a viewpoint of the Natural Bridge, awkwardly located for a really good photograph, but spectacular all the same—about 100 feet high and 100 feet long, it arches over a deep ravine, appearing to defy gravity.

Fog-covered Lake Ethel, center, and Lake James, right

MOWICH LAKE AND CARBON RIVER

19 NORTHERN LOOP TRAIL

Round trip 35 miles (56 km)
Hiking time 4 days
High point 6740 feet

Elevation gain 8500 feet
Snowfree mid-July to mid-October

A long loop hike in the most pristine wilderness of the Park, through forests and meadows, over rivers, under a cliff of colorful rocks, near the Natural Bridge, past numerous mountain lakes, in ever-changing views of The Mountain and its glaciers. The first portion to Lake James can be done as an overnight trip.

Drive to the Carbon River Entrance and continue to road-end at Ipsut Creek Campground, elevation 2300 feet. Find the Wonderland Trail at the upper boundary of the camp.

The first 2 miles follow the valley above the river. At a junction take the left fork across the Carbon River (Hike 18). On the far bank turn left again, downstream a bit. Then begins a series of countless switchbacks, climbing 3000 feet, mostly—a mercy—in cool forest on a smooth and soft path. At 5¼ miles from Ipsut Creek Campground, pass Yellowstone Cliffs campsite. Above the trail are Tyee Peak and the Yellowstone

Cliffs; beside it, a pair of small lakes to the left and another to the right. The tundra of 5800-foot Windy Gap (6 miles from Ipsut Creek) offers wide views, well worth a lengthy lunch stop.

At a few hundred yards beyond the top of Windy Gap is the side-trail to Natural Bridge, a 1¾-mile round trip (Hike 18).

The Northern Loop Trail descends 1400 feet in 2 miles to camps at Lake James, 4370 feet. Here, 8 miles from Ipsut Creek, is the turnaround for overnighters. (If Lake James rather than the complete loop is the aim, it's better to start at Sunrise. The distance is greater but the elevation gain less.)

From Lake James, the route drops to a crossing of the West Fork White River, where a 2500-foot climb begins, at 4½ miles passing a side-trail to Fire Creek Camp. Water is not dependable here; if camping is the plan, fill buckets at Van Horn Falls, near the West Fork. At 6 miles from Lake James is a junction with the Grand Park trail (Hike 28). Continue right another 3 miles to a camp in lower Berkeley Park. Total distance from Lake James, 9 miles.

From Berkeley Park Camp climb 1 mile through meadows to a junction with the Wonderland Trail. Turn right and cross 6740-foot Skyscraper Pass. Descend 800 feet to Granite Creek campsite, 4½ miles from Berkeley Park. From Skyscraper Pass the trail drops a total of 2100 feet to the snout of the Winthrop Glacier and a crossing of Winthrop Creek, a tributary of the White River, then gains 1200 feet to Mystic Camp at 5700 feet, 10 miles from Berkeley Park.

To complete the remaining 8 miles of the loop, the trail climbs 400 feet to a 6100-foot pass and then (as described in Hike 17) descends through Moraine Park, crosses the Carbon River, and returns to the starting point at Ipsut Creek.

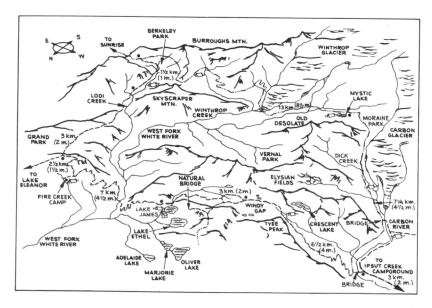

20   OWYHIGH LAKES

Round trip to lakes from White River 7 miles (11 km)
Hiking time 3½ hours
High point 5185 feet
Elevation gain 1350 feet
Snowfree mid-July through October

One way from White River to Deer Creek 8½ miles (13½ km)
Hiking time 5 hours
High point 5400 feet
Elevation gain 2500 feet in, 500 feet out
Snowfree mid-July to mid-October

Alpine lakes surrounded by acres of wildflowers in the shadow of the ragged peaks of Governors Ridge.

There are two ways to reach the lakes: a 3½-mile trail from the White River and a 5-mile trail from the road to Ohanapecosh. If transportation can be arranged, the two can be combined in a one-way hike; the best starting place for such a trip is the White River approach, since going this direction involves slightly less elevation gain.

Drive from the White River Entrance 2 miles to a parking area on the right, 1 mile beyond Shaw Creek, elevation 3750 feet. The trail starts on the left side of the road and climbs steadily through the woods, the path wide and smooth with long switchbacks. At 3 miles, ½ mile short of the lakes, is Tamanos backcountry campsite, the only camp on this trail. Tamanos Creek normally is dry by mid-August. The timber thins shortly before reaching the 5100-foot lakes. To the east is craggy Governors Ridge. Directly west is Tamanos Mountain.

From the lakes the trail climbs another 300 feet to a 5400-foot pass with a view of Cowlitz Chimneys, then drops steadily but not steeply into Kotsuck Creek and down to the junction with the East Side Trail. In

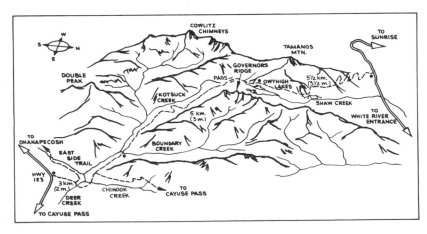

Owyhigh Lake and Governors Ridge

about 2 miles pass a viewpoint of a waterfall. In 3 miles cross Boundary Creek. Take time out to walk up the creek bed to a waterfall.

Save energy for the last ½ mile. At the junction with the East Side Trail, cross Chinook Creek, then Deer Creek, and take the Deer Creek trail, which climbs 400 feet to the highway.

21 SUMMERLAND

Round trip 8½ miles (13½ km)
Hiking time 4 hours
High point 5920 feet

Elevation gain 2100 feet
Snowfree July to October

One of the favorite hikes in the Park, on a wide path to an alpine meadow under the pinnacle of Little Tahoma. For those who don't wish to do the whole trip, the lower portion of the trail makes a fine forest walk. Many deep-woods flowers that by early summer have come and gone on the south side of the Park are just starting to bloom in this valley as late as the middle of August; especially notable is the queen's cup beadlily. This is one of the most crowded areas of the Park, with 300–400 hikers a day.

Drive from the White River Entrance 3 miles to a parking area just beyond the Fryingpan Creek bridge, elevation 3800 feet. The trail starts across the highway.

For 2 miles the way ascends gently in forest to a bluff overlooking Fryingpan Creek. At about 3 miles pass through debris of a large avalanche and cross the creek. The final 1 mile is steep, ending in a series of short switchbacks; here, during July and August, look for attractive displays of avalanche lily.

The stone shelter cabin and backcountry campsites are in the grove to the left. Little Tahoma dominates the meadows, rising above the Fryingpan Glacier to the southwest. West are the Emmons Glacier and Mount

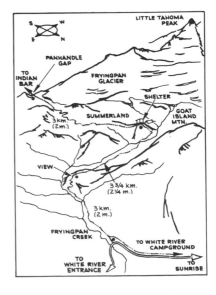

Queen's cup (also called beadlily)

Mountain goats near Panhandle Gap

Rainier. North is Goat Island Mountain. East are the Sarvent Glaciers. South is Panhandle Gap.

If transportation can be arranged, a classic 2–3 day trip is over Panhandle Gap to Indian Bar (Hike 40) and on down to the Box Canyon on the Stevens Canyon Road, a total one-way distance of 17 miles.

From Summerland climb 840 feet in less than 2 miles to 6750-foot Panhandle Gap. A good share of this distance is through rough moraine. From the Gap the trail traverses wintry and barren slopes above Ohanapecosh Park 1½ miles before descending 2 miles to Indian Bar. This is the highest and most desolate section of the Wonderland Trail. Much of the way lies over large snowfields; though the route is marked by a few rock cairns, it is very easy to lose in a fog, not to mention a storm.

Inexperienced hikers should not attempt to travel this area early in the season or in bad weather. After spells of good weather, though, generally the track is clearly booted into the snow and can be followed quite safely if the only problem is a dense fog.

From Indian Bar proceed on out the Cowlitz Divide to Box Canyon.

Panhandle Gap demands a special note. Atop the Gap, look up and left to the Cowlitz Chimneys, volcanic plugs from old eruptions; except on very hot days, there is a fair chance of seeing mountain goats.

Glacier Basin and mountain climbers headed for the summit.

WHITE RIVER

22 GLACIER BASIN

Round trip 7 miles (11 km)
Hiking time 4 hours
High point 6000 feet

Elevation gain 1700 feet
Snowfree July to October

A trip that offers no overwhelming view of The Mountain, but more than compensates with the peaceful seclusion of a meadowy basin. The easy walk also displays artifacts of the Storbo Mine. From here, in

1894–5, "high-grading" prospectors took out ore samples valued by them at $450 a ton. In 1902 a copper claim was established, but despite sporadic speculative activity until 1957, nothing of commercial value was ever found.

Drive from the White River Entrance 5 miles to the White River bridge and turn left on the gravel road to the White River Campground. Find the trail at the upper end of the camp, elevation 4350 feet.

The walking begins—and continues much of the way—on remnants of the miners' old wagon road, which was passable to automobiles as late as the 1940s. The open road is hot on sunny days, but runs close to cool pools of the Inter Fork of the White River.

At 1 mile is a junction with the Emmons Moraine trail, a ½-mile side-trip to a view of the snout of the largest glacier in the conterminous 48 states. One must use imagination to be impressed by the heaps of rubble covering the glacial ice. There is, however, a good view of Little Tahoma rising above.

In 2½ miles pass the remains of the miners' sawmill and power plant. Here the trail leaves what's left of the mine road and climbs steeply into open meadows, then levels off and enters Glacier Basin.

Bands of goats prowl the high slopes. In season the basin floor is bright with flowers. A tiny bit of The Mountain appears above The Wedge, topped by Mt. Ruth and Steamboat Prow. Splendid campsites.

A climbers' track continues from the basin toward Interglacier, rising out of flowers and greenery into bouldery wastes of ice country.

If transportation can be arranged, Glacier Basin can be reached by an easy downhill trail from Sunrise (Hike 30), one-way hikers then going on out to the White River Campground.

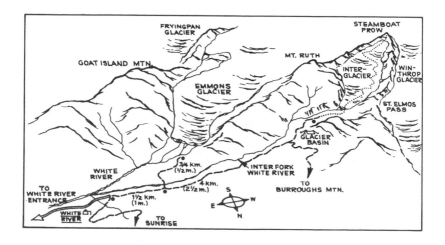

23 PALISADES LAKES

Round trip 7 miles (11 km)
Hiking time 4 hours
High point 6150 feet

Elevation gain 700 feet in, 900 feet out
Snowfree mid-July to mid-October

A series of at least seven lakes along the trail, all on the "dry" side of the mountain. No views of The Mountain, but an interesting rock formation called The Palisades. The trail has one bad feature: it drops 500 feet and then goes up and down, up and down.

Drive from the White River Entrance 10½ miles to the parking area at Sunrise Point. Cross the highway on the north side and look over the stone railing directly down at Sunrise Lake, the first of the series. The trail starts at the north end of the horseshoe bend, elevation 6150 feet.

The way follows the ridge down a short distance, then switchbacks toward Sunrise Lake. In ½ mile the trail divides. The left fork leads to Sunrise Lake, the choice of most hikers and a good destination for a short walk. However, more and better lakes lie beyond, so take the right fork.

In 1½ miles from the road the path skirts Clover Lake, largest of the chain. At 2½ miles pass Tom, Dick, and Harry Lakes (campsite at Dick) and a side-trail to Hidden Lake. The main trail ends in another mile at Upper Palisades Lake.

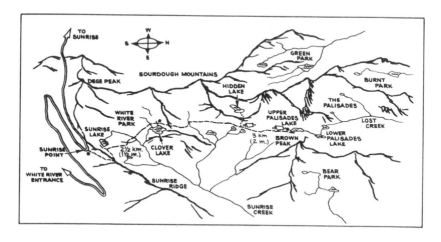

Palisades Lake

Little Tahoma and Emmons Glacier from Shadow Lake

WHITE RIVER

24 SUNRISE NATURE TRAILS

**Round trip from ½ to 4 miles (¾ to
  6½ km)**
**Snowfree mid-July through
  September**

A glacier overlook, a walk high above the White River through a silver forest with views directly down on White River Campground, and a gem of a lake. Drive from the White River Entrance to Sunrise and take as many of these hikes as time and energy permit.

Sourdough Ridge Nature Trail:

A self-guiding nature trail, starting on the north side of the picnic area and going in a loop, an easy hour's stroll, through meadows and along the ridge to fine views of Rainier and down to Huckleberry Park.

Emmons Vista Nature Trail:

Find the ½-mile trail directly across the parking lot from Sunrise Lodge, near the gravel road to the campground. At the start is a box containing copies of an interpretive pamphlet keyed to numbered posts along the way. At the end of the trail is an exhibit explaining the workings of a glacier.

Silver Forest:

From Sunrise walk the Emmons Vista trail a short bit to the start of the Silver Forest trail. The way is fairly level, traversing the brow of the hill above the White River valley. Views of The Mountain are unlimited; the silver forest, trees killed by fire and bleached by weather, offers picturesque foregrounds. Mountain bluebirds make their homes in the snags.

Sunrise Rim Trail:

At a junction in the Emmons Vista trail, turn right and contour along a steep hillside with views of The Mountain and White River. Pass junction with the Wonderland Trail which drops 3 miles to the White River. Shadow Lake is surrounded by groves of alpine trees and flowers in season. Views of Little Tahoma, though Mount Rainier is hidden. The lake is only a few feet from the hike-in campground. Return by the trail or the closed road.

A considerably more energetic (but worth it) alternate return is via the high trail visible up on the Sourdough Mountains. Follow the road and signs for the Wonderland Trail (west) from the campground back toward Sunrise. The way climbs steeply to Frozen Lake, the fenced water supply for facilities at Sunrise. After climbing 500 feet in less than ½ mile, reach the Wonderland Trail and pass below the lake. Walk a long 1 mile over a hump and along a sidehill, then drop through meadows to Sunrise.

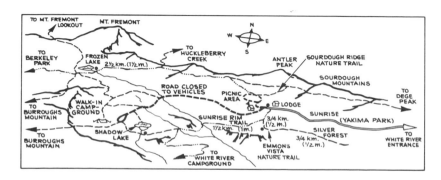

SOURDOUGH TRAIL

Round trip 4 miles (6½ km)
Hiking time 2 hours
High point 7006 feet

Elevation gain 600 feet
Snowfree mid-July through
September

An alpine ridge with a classic view of Mount Rainier. Look down on Sunrise Lodge and the busy highway. End at Sunrise Point parking lot. Along the way take a spur trail to the top of Dege Peak for a broad panorama of Cascade Crest summits.

Drive from the White River Entrance to Sunrise, elevation 6385 feet. Sourdough Mountains are the long ridge of low peaks rising to the north. The trail leaves from the picnic area at a large sign. In a short distance pass a junction. Keep right, following signs for Dege Peak.

Soon the trail is joined by a rehabilitated, steep shortcut from the lodge. This latter was not built, but was the result of countless impatient hikers shortcutting the well-graded path. Thousands of hours of work by rangers and the Youth Conservation Corps have gone into replanting and restoring the shortcut to meadow.

The views get better and the crowds thinner the farther one goes out the ridge. The path stays near the crest, contouring around the higher summits. Where the track starts up Dege Peak, keep left at a junction for the final short bit to the top.

Horizons are unlimited. Mount Rainier is supreme, of course, but still must compete with the Sarvent Glaciers and Cowlitz Chimneys to the south. Far below is the White River and US 410, the highway over Chinook Pass. Farther north rise distant peaks of the Cascades and northwest are the Olympic Mountains. At the east base of the peak lie Sunrise and Clover Lakes (Hike 23), and on the northwest slopes are the green meadows of Huckleberry Park.

If transportation can be arranged, go back the short bit to the junction and take the trail 1 mile down the ridge to Sunrise Point. However, if such an opportunity is available, it's more interesting to walk from Sunrise Point to Sunrise; this way the view is always in front. The trail

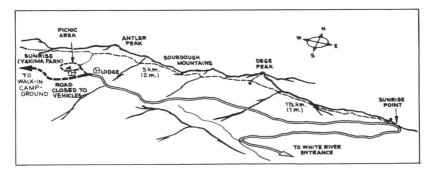

Mount Rainier from Sourdough Mountain trail

starts on the uphill side of the highway from the parking area and follows the ridge. The Sunrise Point beginning adds 300 feet of elevation to the climb but the one-way hiking distance is only 3 miles instead of the 4-mile round trip from Sunrise Lodge.

Huckleberry Creek

26 HUCKLEBERRY CREEK

One way 10 miles (16 km)
Hiking time (downhill) 4 hours
High point 6700 feet

Elevation gain 200 feet, loss 3600 feet
Snowfree mid-July through September

Miles of forest walking within sound of the clear bubbling water of Huckleberry Creek, passing by numerous waterfalls, Forest Lake amid the trees, and finally a meadow basin and alpine ridge—a superb approach from low country to high country and one of the wildest and most respectful ways to experience the Park from bottom to top.

However, the trail (which probably predates the Park) was built by men in a hurry to get places and is very steep. Therefore, many hikers prefer to have their dessert first and then the main course and the soup and salad—which is to say, they start at the top in Yakima Park and descend to the bottom at the Huckleberry Creek road in Mount Baker-Snoqualmie National Forest.

To do the one-way downhill trip, transportation must be arranged. Such as, drive in two cars from Enumclaw on US 410 to a junction with Forest Service road No. 73 and continue right 5½ miles, then onto road No. 7340 almost to its end, elevation 3000 feet. Leave one car at a small parking lot near Forest Service trail No. 1182, which is supposed to be signed "Huckleberry Creek Trail—Park Boundary 1½ Miles." However, as of 1988 the Forest Service's end of the trail was **not** signed; a map may be needed to find it. In the second car, drive to the White River Entrance and on to Sunrise, elevation 6385 feet.

Begin walking from the picnic area, as for Sourdough Mountains (Hike 25). In a short bit climb left on the Wonderland Trail ½ mile to the ridge crest and a junction. Go right, dropping rapidly in a series of short switchbacks to a divide between an attractive meadow basin on the right and a cold and rocky cirque on the left. The trail switchbacks down into the cirque, crosses a tumbling headwater of Huckleberry Creek, swings around a shoulder to a second headwater, then falls into forest and 5653-foot Forest Lake, with one backcountry campsite.

The grade moderates a bit below the lake, but the next 3 miles still are pretty stiff. The lower reaches of the trail follow creek meanders along the valley bottom. At the Park boundary is an old patrol cabin fenced by huge windfalls which have missed it by inches; one year this relic of the past will be the target of a toppling tree.

The bottom-to-top-and-back-again round-trip 20 miles can be done without special transportation arrangements on a weekend backpack. Those who earn the high meadows by hiking the valley approach get some notion of how glorious it was to enter Yakima Park when it was wild; they pity travelers who arrive in automobiles.

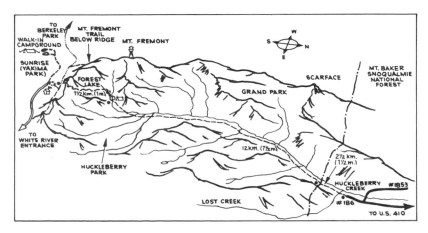

27 MT. FREMONT LOOKOUT

Round trip 5½ miles (9 km)
Hiking time 3 hours
High point 7200 feet

Elevation gain 800 feet
Snowfree mid-July through
** September**

A fire lookout with the white glaciers of Mount Rainier on one side and the greenery of National Park and National Forest trees on the other.

Drive from the White River Entrance to Sunrise, elevation 6385 feet. From the picnic area walk the old Wonderland Trail route upward ⅓ mile, then go left to Frozen Lake and a meeting of five trails at 1½ miles. The lookout trail follows the west side of Frozen Lake and climbs around the hill to the north. The highest point of the trail is at the ridge corner. From here the way descends a bit as it traverses ½ mile to the lookout, which is not on the summit of Mt. Fremont.

South is The Mountain, north the long line of Cascades. On a clear day the Olympics appear, and with binoculars one can see the Space Needle in Seattle.

Closer are the flat expanse of Grand Park (Hike 28) and, beyond, the forests. Logging roads are being built by the Forest Service almost to the Park boundary; eventually the only virgin forest remaining will be that within the Park.

The lookout is occupied during periods of extreme fire danger. If a ranger is on duty, he or she will be glad to explain duties and show how the fire-locator works. Ask the ranger to point out the Natural Bridge on the Northern Loop (Hike 18); it appears quite small from here, but is visible when the sun is right.

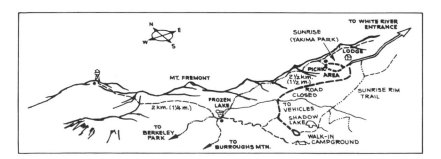

Mount Fremont Lookout

28 GRAND PARK

Round trip to Grand Park 13 miles (21 km)
Hiking time 6 hours
High point 6700 feet

Elevation gain 700 feet in, 1500 feet out
Snowfree mid-July through September

In the up-and-down landscape of Mount Rainier, the almost flat 2-mile-long plateau of Grand Park is a striking oddity. The explanation: many millennia ago a lava flow filled an ancient canyon; the displaced streams sought new courses at the edges of the flow, leaving the lava surface as a high tableland, which was later covered by a thick layer of pumice. A small herd of elk makes its home here, and chances are good of seeing a genuinely "wild" (unaccustomed to humans) bear. An immense collection of flowers.

Drive from the White River Entrance to Sunrise, elevation 6385 feet. From the picnic area follow the Wonderland Trail (west) 1½ miles to a five-way junction. Continue on the Wonderland Trail west, across and down a pretty and varied series of meadows. In a little over ½ mile is another junction. Keep right and follow the Northern Loop Trail, dropping rapidly into Berkeley Park. Pass a series of springs (oozing ground, green lush plants). In lower Berkeley Park are loud and lovely waterfalls of Lodi Creek, a talus where marmots whistle from boulders. At 4 miles from Sunrise is Berkeley Park backcountry campsite.

The way descends in forest to 5200 feet, a total elevation loss from Frozen Lake of 1500 feet, which must be regained on the return. Then the trail swings out of the valley onto a dividing ridge between trees of Lodi Creek and meadows of Cold Basin and climbs 300 feet to the edge of Grand Park, elevation about 5600 feet, 6¼ miles from Sunrise. The Mt. Fremont lookout can be seen above.

The trail continues ¾ mile across meadows to a junction. The Northern Loop Trail drops 2 miles to Fire Creek Camp. Go right a minimum of another ¼ mile for a unique view of Mount Rainier rising above Grand Park.

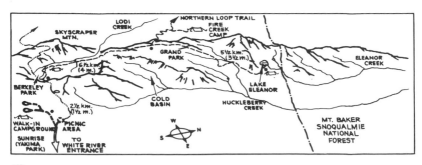

Grand Park and Mount Rainier

Lake Eleanor is another ½ mile across Grand Park. The trail, marked by posts, descends 400 feet in woods to the lake, on the edge of the Park at 4985 feet. Good camping. The stillness, however, may be broken by the roar of logging trucks on a Forest Service road less than ¾ mile away.

29 SKYSCRAPER PASS

Round trip 7 miles (11 km)
Hiking time 4 hours
High point 6773 feet

Elevation gain 900 feet in, 300 feet out
Snowfree mid-July through September

Miles of alpine meadows are the main attraction of this high section of the Wonderland Trail. However, the flowers must compete with views north along the Cascade Range and the bits and pieces of Mount Rainier that rise above surrounding ridges.

Drive from the White River Entrance to the road-end at Sunrise, elevation 6385 feet. From the picnic area follow the Wonderland-Sourdough Ridge trail upward ⅓ mile and then go left toward Frozen Lake. Five different trails come together near the lake; go straight ahead on the Wonderland Trail, headed west toward Mystic Lake and the Carbon River.

From Frozen Lake the way descends 300 feet to a junction with the Northern Loop-Berkeley Park trail. Stay left, contouring high above the green meadows of Berkeley Park, and then climb to 6700-foot Skyscraper Pass and views down Granite Creek to the snout of the Winthrop Glacier and across the valley to Old Desolate, Sluiskin Mountain, and the green meadows of remote, seldom-visited Vernal Park.

The ground at Skyscraper Pass, composed of pumice, is extremely fragile, and vegetation is scarce. Wool hanging on stunted trees is evidence that a large number of mountain goats groom themselves here.

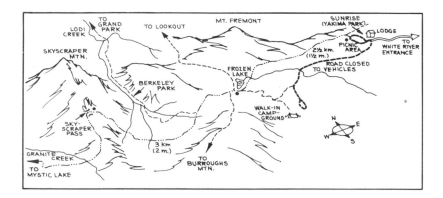

Skyscraper Mountain

30 BURROUGHS MOUNTAIN

**Round trip to Second Burroughs 5
   miles (8 km)
Hiking time 3 hours
High point 7400 feet**

**Elevation gain 1200 feet
Snowfree late July through
   September**

If there is a trail between earth and heaven, this is it. The ridge of Burroughs Mountain, high above the White River, gives the impression of going easily onward and upward to the very tip of Columbia Crest.

Any part of the walk is superb, and the first section usually is crowded with travelers aged from less than 1 year to more than 70. As one goes along, the crowds dwindle.

Note: Belying the benignity of the meadows, the trail crosses a steep snowfield that doesn't melt until August—or some years at all. Before setting out, ask the ranger about this killer snowfield—and also about its twin on the trail up from Frozen Lake, described below.

Mount Rainier from First Burroughs Mountain

Drive from the White River Entrance to Sunrise, elevation 6385 feet. The trail starts on the south side of the parking lot and goes to the walk-in Sunrise Campground.

From the campground the trail makes a stiff little climb to an overlook of the White River and Emmons Glacier—a good turnaround for short-trippers—then continues up around a slope of slabby chunks of andesite (and the snowfield that lingers late) onto a wide, flat plateau. Burroughs Mountain, like Grand Park (Hike 28), is the remnant of a lava flow which filled an ancient canyon; the displaced streams carved valleys at the sides of the flow, leaving a tableland as yet relatively undissected. In 2½ miles is the 7300-foot high point of First Burroughs Mountain and the junction with the trail from Frozen Lake.

Another ½ mile leads to 7400-foot Second Burroughs and a memorial to Edmond S. Meany, long-time president of The Mountaineers. No water on the high ridge, but despite that, small flowers and clumps of heather are strewn through the volcanic rubble. North is the odd, green plateau of Grand Park. West are views toward the Carbon Glacier and Moraine Park.

Burroughs Mountain offers possibly the finest easily-accessible tundra in the Cascades. This plant community grows very, very slowly. The thin volcanic soil contains little nourishment, and moisture is not held long for plants to use. The growing season is short. Strong winds dry the plants and sandblast the vegetation with pumice.

In addition to struggling with these difficult environmental factors, this alpine vegetation is sometimes subjected to man's impact. Hiking off the trail causes crushing and breaking of plants, destroys seeds for future plant crops, and can reduce the small amount of organic matter in the thin topsoil. Moving rocks to make cairns or windbreaks exposes roots to drying and eventual death. Studies have shown that recovery from such stresses takes hundreds of years, even after all off-trail hiking is halted.

To vary the return, take the Wonderland Trail back to Sunrise via Frozen Lake (Hike 27). The distance is about the same as the other approach, and the views down into the greenery of Berkeley Park have a dreamlike quality. However, as noted above, a steep snow slope makes this route unsafe until mid-August or so.

From Second Burroughs Mountain the trail descends 2¼ miles to the Glacier Basin trail (Hike 22), reaching it at a point ¾ mile from the basin and 2½ miles from the road at White River Campground.

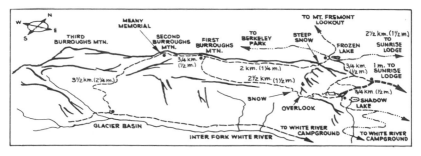

Upper Crystal Lake

31 CRYSTAL LAKES

Round trip 6 miles (9½ km)
Hiking time 3 hours
High point 5836 feet

Elevation gain 2300 feet
Snowfree mid-June through
October

Crystal-clear water surrounded by alpine flower fields. Elk are sometimes seen. And frequently dogs, more of a problem here than just about anywhere in the Park.

Drive east from Enumclaw on US 410 to the National Park boundary and continue 4½ miles to State Highway Department maintenance sheds, elevation 3500 feet. Park near here, but stay out of the workmen's way; they need most of the space for their machines. Find the trail close to where Crystal Creek goes into a culvert.

After a steady climb through forest, at a little more than 1½ miles the trail crosses the base of an avalanche slope, up which it then makes a couple of long switchbacks. The third crossing gives the best look at The Mountain, which disappears after that behind Crystal Peak (not to be confused with Crystal Mountain). In about 1 mile from the avalanche pass lower Crystal Lake, and in ½ mile more reach the 5830-foot upper and larger lake.

A number of elk and mountain goat make their summer home in this area. Look for them on slopes around the upper lake. Note the rock formations to the east; through at least two windows in the rocks blue sky can be seen.

For better views of The Mountain, climb to the old lookout site on Crystal Peak. Find the unmaintained trail at the end of a switchback about 1¼ miles from the highway.

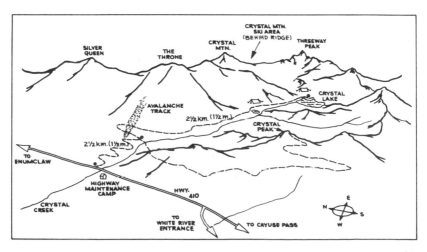

32 NACHES PEAK LOOP

Loop trip 4½ miles (7 km)
Hiking time 3 hours
High point 6000 feet

Elevation gain 700 feet
Snowfree mid-July through
October

An easy loop hike circling one of the guardians of Chinook Pass, passing through rich flower fields and beside two lakelets. Superb views of Rainier. Blueberries (usually) by late September. A magnificence of flaming color in autumn.

Drive east from Enumclaw on US 410 to Chinook Pass and park, elevation 5040 feet.

The loop can be done in either direction, but going clockwise keeps Mount Rainier in front more of the time and thus is recommended. However, until late July or early August the trail along the east slopes of Naches Peak is quite snowy; unless a party is equipped for snow travel, it may prefer to set out on the counterclockwise circuit, turning back when the country becomes too white and wet for personal tastes. In such case, park at Tipsoo Lake.

To start the clockwise loop at Chinook Pass, intersect the Pacific Crest Trail and follow it south over the highway on the wooden overpass. Small paths branch off left and right; stay on the main grade along the east side of Naches Peak, leaving the National Park and entering the William O. Douglas Wilderness.

The way traverses a steep sidehill above a green little valley, crossing several small waterfall-tumbling creeks—which, however, generally dry up in August. Flowers are at their prime roughly from late July to early August, but some bloom earlier, some later. About 1 mile from Chinook Pass is an unnamed lakelet.

From the lakelet the trail ascends gently over a ridge, which is the highest point of the loop, enters the Park, and at 2 miles reaches a junction. The Pacific Crest Trail goes left, dropping to Dewey Lakes (excellent camping; see Hike 33).

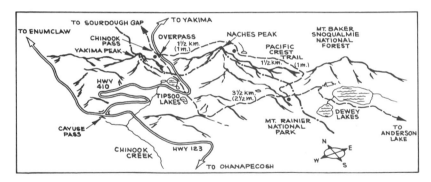

Mount Rainier from south side of Naches Peak

The loop trail goes right, over a small rise to another unnamed lakelet reflecting Rainier. The way winds to high meadows on the west side of Naches Peak, Mount Rainier always in full view, and drops back to the highway near Upper Tipsoo Lake, ½ mile from the starting point.

The Naches Peak loop is among the most popular hikes in the Park. Even more popular, and a pleasure for anyone who can walk at all, no matter how slowly, are the two beginning and ending segments, which in a few hundred feet or any longer distance offer as nice a combination of flower-sniffing and mountain-gazing as one can find anywhere.

For a whole new experience of high meadows and The Mountain, do the loop on a moonlit night in late August or early September. Listen for the bugling of bull elk.

Dewey Lakes and shoulder of Seymour Peak

33 PACIFIC CREST TRAIL– DEWEY LAKES

One way from Chinook Pass to Ohanapecosh Highway 18 miles (29 km)
Hiking time 2–3 days
High point 5800 feet
Elevation gain 1500 feet
Elevation loss 5100 feet
Snowfree mid-July through October

Round trip to Dewey Lakes 5 miles (8 km)
Hiking time 3 hours
High point 5800 feet
Elevation gain 400 feet in, 700 feet out

The Pacific Crest Trail extends from Canada to Mexico and in 1968 was acknowledged as an American classic when Congress gave it status as a National Scenic Trail.

The portion of the Crest Trail running along the east boundary of the Park (with frequent swings out into the William O. Douglas Wilderness) goes up and down, sometimes in subalpine forest but mostly in meadows, passing numerous lakes and ponds, waterfalls and flower fields. Occasional views of Mount Rainier and other views to peaks and valleys of the Wilderness.

Whether a group is planning to hike this entire segment of the Crest Trail or only to Dewey Lakes, the best starting point is 5040-foot Chinook Pass—rather than the 1900-foot trailhead deep in the Ohanapecosh valley. (Good access is also available from White Pass on National Forest land.) To do the one-way hike recommended, transportation must be arranged.

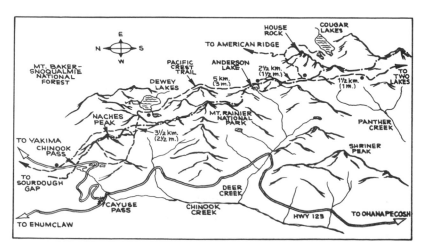

Pacific Crest Trail—Dewey Lakes (Continued)

Drive US 410 east from Enumclaw or west from Yakima to Chinook Pass and park east of the summit. Go south on the Pacific Crest Trail, cross the highway on the wooden overpass, enter the William O. Douglas Wilderness, and in a scant 2 miles swing briefly through Mount Rainier National Park to the Naches Loop trail (Hike 32) junction.

Keep left, reenter the Wilderness, and descend 700 feet in a long ½ mile to Dewey Lakes, 5100 feet. Good campsites at both lakes, which are outside the Park. Forest Service camping permits are required. Camping is banned within 100 feet of the water. The lakes make a fine destination for beginning hikers and small children; the round-trip distance from Chinook Pass is only 5 miles, an easy weekend.

From Dewey Lakes the trail climbs past a wide meadow-marsh laced with meandering streams, then rounds a shoulder of Seymour Peak. At 5½ miles is little Anderson Lake, with meadowy shores and forests on all sides. This is a good turnaround for a long day's round trip from Chinook Pass.

The trail climbs steeply a few hundred feet from Anderson Lake and reenters the Park for ¼ mile in the headwaters of Deer Creek, with views of Mount Rainier, then drops a bit, leaves the Park, and at 7 miles reaches a junction with the American Ridge-Cougar Lakes trail. Back in the Park again, switchbacks climb the forested west side of House Rock into flowers again. At 9½ miles the way leaves the Park, crosses the crest, and contours above Two Lakes. At 10 miles a side-trail drops 300 feet to campsites at Two Lakes (no camping permit needed). The Crest Trail continues south and again slips briefly into the Park and out. At 11

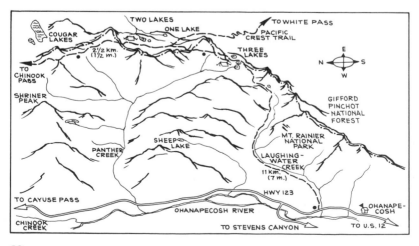

Deer near Two Lakes

miles is a junction. The Pacific Crest Trail leaves the Park for good and continues south 15 miles to White Pass. Keep right (straight ahead) and descend 1 mile to Three Lakes backcountry campsites (camping permit needed; Hike 36) and 6 miles more to the highway near Ohanapecosh.

34 EAST SIDE TRAIL

**One way from Deer Creek to
Ohanapecosh 9 miles (14½ km)
Hiking time 4 hours**

**High point 3500 feet
Elevation loss 1500 feet
Snowfree June to mid-November**

A forest hike near a cool river. Try it in spring when higher trails are still buried under snow or in summer when The Mountain is lost in rain or in late fall when meadowlands are a blank misery of cold-blowing storm. A wide path with little brush to moisturize clothing.

If transportation can be arranged, this is an ideal one-way trip. Start at the top and walk downhill; except for the first ½ mile, the grade is so gentle a hiker hardly is aware of descending.

Drive the East Side Highway north 6 miles from the Stevens Canyon Entrance, or south 5 miles from Cayuse Pass, to a very small parking space ½ mile south of Deer Creek. Sign on the west side of the road. Elevation, 3232 feet.

The trail drops rapidly a scant ½ mile to a nice campsite at the junction of Deer Creek and Chinook Creek. Here the way is joined by the East Side Trail, descending from Cayuse Pass and Chinook Pass. (For an even longer one-way hike, pick up this trail at either pass and follow it on down; to the total one-way distance add 5½ miles from Chinook, 4 miles from Cayuse.)

In 1 mile from Deer Creek cross Chinook Creek above a pretty canyon and falls. In about 3 miles cross the Ohanapecosh over a corkscrew of a falls. About 6½ miles pass a side-trail to the Grove of the Patriarchs (Hike 37). In a little over 7 miles cross the Stevens Canyon Road and in another ½ mile join the Silver Falls trail (Hike 38) and hike either side of the river into Ohanapecosh Campground.

Mostly the walk is out of sight of the river, but never out of sound. Sometimes the way is through virgin forest, occasionally crossing an avalanche slope covered with vine maple.

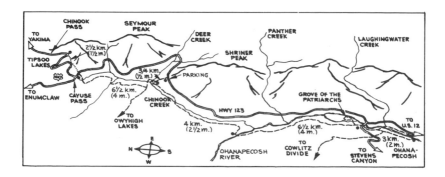

Trail bridge across Chinook Creek

35 SHRINER PEAK

Round trip to Shriner Peak 8
  miles (12¾ km)
Hiking time 5 hours

High point 5834 feet
Elevation gain 3434 feet
Snowfree July through October

A lookout peak with a commanding view of the Ohanapecosh valley and Mount Rainier, and distant views of the Cascades north and south. A meadow lake in a basin below, summer home of a large herd of elk. Despite the panoramas this is one of the loneliest trails in the Park.

Drive north on the East Side Highway 3½ miles from the Stevens Canyon Entrance, or south 7½ miles from Cayuse Pass, to the parking area on the west side of the road about ½ mile north of the Panther Creek bridge. The trail and sign are on the east side of the road, both almost hidden from sight. Elevation is 2400 feet.

On sunny days it is best to start early in the morning to beat the heat. The dusty trail swings steeply from cool forest to hot hillside, climbing through an old burn with trees too small to give much shade. In 2½ miles the way reaches the crest of a ridge; still no shade, but the view—and possible breeze—make the rest of the hike bearable. The last 1 mile switchbacks to the 5834-foot summit and the lookout building, which is seldom staffed.

Camping is permitted near the top of Shriner Peak. Water may have to be hauled some distance. Campers definitely will want to get up at dawn to watch the sunrise on Rainier's shining glaciers.

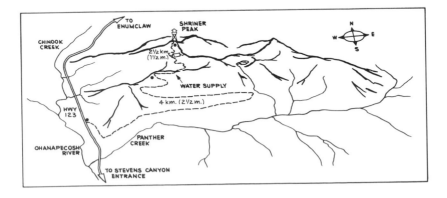

Air view of Shriner Peak and Mount Rainier

36 LAUGHINGWATER CREEK– THREE LAKES TRAIL

Round trip to Three Lakes 12 miles (19 km)
Hiking time 6 hours

High point 5000 feet
Elevation gain 2700 feet
Snowfree July through October

A woods trail to three small lakes and onward to the Pacific Crest Trail. Or a loitering mile through moss-covered forest to a picnic spot beside the laughing water.

Drive about 1 mile north from Ohanapecosh, or a scant mile south from the Stevens Canyon Entrance, to Laughingwater Creek. Park on the west shoulder of the highway north of the creek, elevation 2150 feet. Trail starts on the east side of the road just beyond a steep bank.

The first 1 mile, the tread smooth and grade gentle, climbs over a small knoll and drops a few inches. For those wanting a short walk this is the turnaround. But before going back, go down to the creek—loud but soothing, not "noise" but the sound of wildness.

The next 2 miles the way climbs gently; water is scarce in late summer. Gradually the trail becomes steeper, crossing a small creek at about 3½ miles.

At 5½ miles pass to the right of the unmarked junction of the abandoned and hard-to-find Boundary Trail. A few feet beyond, on the left, is the abandoned 3-mile-long Sheep Lake (a small pond) trail, also very difficult to follow. Neither trail ever was much used.

From the Sheep Lake junction the Laughingwater trail drops slightly

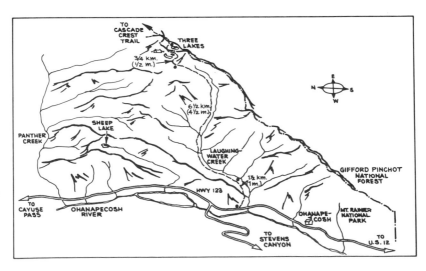

to 4850-foot Three Lakes and backcountry campsites at 6 miles from the road. The patrol cabin, a log structure, is in a picturesque setting between the first and second lakes. Nearby is the camp area.

Follow the trail along the middle lake a few hundred feet to the Park boundary and the third lake. Continue ½ mile, climbing from trees into open country. For views of Mount Rainier hike another 1 mile to the junction with the Pacific Crest Trail (Hike 33).

Patrol cabin at Three Lakes

37 GROVE OF THE PATRIARCHS

Round trip 1½ miles (2½ km)   **Snowfree June through October**
Hiking time 1 hour
High point 2200 feet
Elevation gain none

The name tells the story: a virgin forest of ancient Douglas-firs, western hemlocks, and western red cedars, a place to become humble in the presence of living things that were already aged—by human measure—when the Normans conquered England. Short and easy walk along a nature trail.

Drive to the Stevens Canyon Entrance and continue ¼ mile on the Stevens Canyon Road to a large parking lot beyond the Ohanapecosh River bridge. Trail starts behind the restrooms. Elevation, 2200 feet.

The way goes upstream through beautiful forest ½ mile to a junction. The nature trail turns right, across a suspension bridge onto an island in the Ohanapecosh River. After passing through small trees, the path forks: go either way; it's a loop. Signs identify plants and describe features of the ecological community.

Isolated on the island and thus protected from fire, the trees have grown to gigantic proportions. In this small area are 20 western red cedars more than 25 feet in circumference; among them is the largest cedar in the Park. There are ten Douglas-firs over 25 feet in circumference; one is 35 feet. The trees are estimated to be nearly 1000 years old.

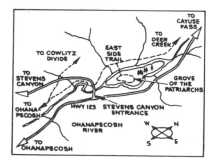

Giant cedar tree in Grove of the Patriarchs

(opposite) Grove of the Patriarchs

38 SILVER FALLS

Loop trip 3 miles (5 km)
Hiking time 1½ hours
High point 2100 feet

Elevation gain 300 feet
Snowfree May through November

Tall virgin forest, a moss-carpeted floor, and a busy waterfall in the Ohanapecosh River. All on an easy loop hike up the east bank of the river, returning down the west side of the valley.

Drive into the Ohanapecosh Campground and park in front of the Visitor Center, elevation 1950 feet. The trail starts behind the center on the Ohanapecosh Hot Springs Nature Trail. In ¼ mile is a junction; go right on the Silver Falls trail, passing hot springs that years ago supported a health resort.

An easy grade follows within sound, if not sight, of the Ohanapecosh River, crossing Laughingwater Creek and climbing over a small bluff to a view of Silver Falls. (If the falls are one's only interest, they can be reached more quickly by taking the Laughingwater Trail from the highway, starting at a point 300 feet north of the Laughingwater Bridge.)

At the falls the loop trail bridges a narrow rock-walled canyon, crossing from the east side of the river to the west. Look down into a deep, crystal-clear pool. The way continues upstream to a scenic overlook at the top of the falls, then a few steps more to a junction with the East Side Trail (Hike 34). Keep left to another junction within a hundred steps. Keep left again. The trail, though now headed downstream, climbs a bit before descending to the starting point.

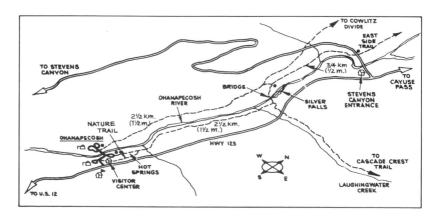

Silver Falls on the Ohanapecosh River

39 COWLITZ DIVIDE

Round trip 8 miles (12¾ km)
Hiking time 4 hours
High point 4760 feet

Elevation gain 2440 feet
Snowfree July through
September

Climb in deep-shadowed virgin forest to a junction with the Wonderland Trail. The route is often used, in combination with the Owyhigh Lakes trail (Hike 20) and East Side Trail (Hike 34), by hikers doing the Wonderland Trail but wishing to avoid the high, snowy country of Panhandle Gap (Hike 21).

Drive from the Stevens Canyon Entrance less than a mile on the Stevens Canyon Road to a parking area and trail sign on the right, elevation 2350 feet.

(The hike can also begin at Ohanapecosh Campground, though this adds 2 miles each way: from the campground follow the Silver Falls trail on the east side of the river, Hike 38; at the falls, cross the footbridge; in a few steps take a left fork and go 300 feet to another junction; take the right fork and in ¼ mile reach the Stevens Canyon Road at the parking area.)

The first 1 mile from the parking area is very moderate, gaining 400 feet through large trees. After a huge log bridge over a small creek, the way steepens, crossing Olallie Creek (campsites nearby) in about 3 miles and in another 1 mile joining the Wonderland Trail a bit before it begins the long drop into Nickel Creek. No mountain views at this turnaround point, but the forest is reward enough.

If transportation can be arranged, a one-way trip can be made, continuing on out Nickel Creek (Hike 40).

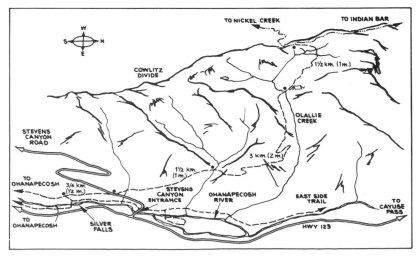

Bridge on Cowlitz Divide trail

40 INDIAN BAR

Round trip 14½ miles (23½ km)
Allow 2 days
High point 5914 feet

Elevation gain 2900 feet in, 800
feet out
Snowfree late July through
September

A unique section of the Wonderland Trail. Miles of ridge-walking through alpine meadows with views of the southeast side of Mount Rainier, ending in a broad green valley into which pour a dozen waterfalls. One of the legendary places in the Park. A great spot to sit in the moonlight on a late-August night and listen to the bull elk bugling.

Drive the Stevens Canyon Road west from the Stevens Canyon Entrance (10 miles), or east 11 miles from the Longmire-Paradise road, to the parking lot at Box Canyon, elevation 3050 feet. Find the signed gravel trail directly across the highway from the parking area. (Do not take the paved nature trail by mistake.)

The first 1 mile is easy walking on a moderate grade to Nickel Creek. Good campsites along the stream and on the far bank. In another ½ mile is a small creek, the last water before Indian Bar. From Nickel Creek the way climbs steadily to the Cowlitz Divide, reaching the crest in a bit less than 3 miles from the road. Here are junctions with the abandoned Backbone Ridge trail and the trail from Ohanapecosh (Hike 39).

The next 4½ miles are along the crest of the Cowlitz Divide, going up and over some bumps and contouring around others. At times the way is very steep. First there are glimpses of The Mountain through trees. Then the trail climbs higher, the meadows grow larger, and finally, atop a 5914-foot knoll, The Mountain comes completely and grandly into the open. To the southeast is Bald Knob. Beyond is Shriner Peak. From the knoll the trail drops 800 feet to 5120-foot Indian Bar.

The Ohanapecosh River divides the large green meadow. The shelter cabin is on the west side of the river. At the valley head are small rem-

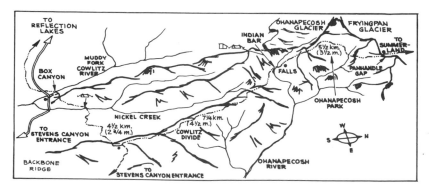

Trail shelter at Indian Bar

nants of the Ohanapecosh Glacier. In early summer numerous waterfalls splash down the lava cliffs. Just 100 feet below the shelter is Wauhaukaupauken Falls, a name almost larger than the falls.

Don't forget the considerable elevation gain on the return hike.

If transportation can be arranged, Indian Bar can be combined with Summerland (Hike 21) for a one-way trip of 17 miles, and a beauty.

41 BENCH AND SNOW LAKES

Round trip 2½ miles (3½ km)
Hiking time 1 hour
High point 4678 feet

Elevation gain 400 feet in, 300 feet out
Snowfree July through October

A trail with three major ups and downs, very dusty in dry weather, traversing shrubby meadows which some years have a spectacular display of beargrass and in the autumn offer the varied reds of mountain-ash and huckleberries.

Drive the Stevens Canyon Road west from the Stevens Canyon Entrance 16 miles or east 3 miles from the Longmire-Paradise road, to a parking area (elevation 4550 feet) about 1 mile east of Louise Lake. Find the trail here.

The two lakes lie at about the same elevation as the parking lot, but several low ridges must be crossed to get there.

Bench Lake, at ¾ mile, lies on the edge of a cliff amid dense thickets of slide alder.

In another ½ mile is Snow Lake, with two of the most beautiful back-country campsites in the Park. The lake occupies a cirque below Unicorn Peak. Shaded by high ridges, snow stays late. Around the shores are open meadows and groups of subalpine fir. To see Mount Rainier, walk to the far side. The lake frequently doesn't melt free of snow until late July. Unicorn Peak, highest point of the Tatoosh Range at 6939 feet, rises directly to the south.

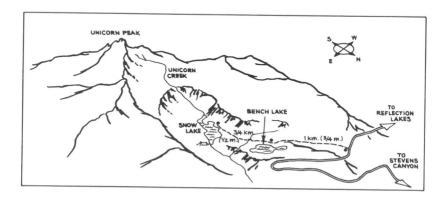

Snow Lake and Unicorn Peak

PINNACLE SADDLE

Round trip 3 miles (5 km)
Hiking time 2–3 hours
High point 6000 feet

Elevation gain 1150 feet
Snowfree August through
September

A grand view of The Mountain, from a point far enough away to see it all in a single wide-eyed look, close enough to see fine detail of glaciers and lava cliffs.

Drive the Stevens Canyon Road west from the Stevens Canyon Entrance 17½ miles or east 1½ miles from the Longmire-Paradise road, to the Reflection Lakes parking area, elevation 4860 feet. The trail starts on the uphill (south) side.

The path is gentle at first, but soon turns steep and remains so. In July several hazardous snowfields must be crossed. Use extreme caution; hikers lacking good boots would do better to give up and try again later in the season, when the snow has melted.

The view of Mount Rainier grows steadily more impressive with every inch of elevation gained; at the 6000-foot saddle is an almost equally impressive view south—across miles of forest, the village of Packwood, and the Goat Rocks—to Mt. Adams.

The trail ends at the saddle. Yet countless tourists, many in street shoes, continue to the top of 6562-foot Pinnacle Peak. Though trained climbers consider Pinnacle an easy ascent, most of the hikers who visit the summit have no business on the steep, unstable rock. They are a hazard to themselves with their slippery shoes—and a hazard to others below as they kick down loose stones.

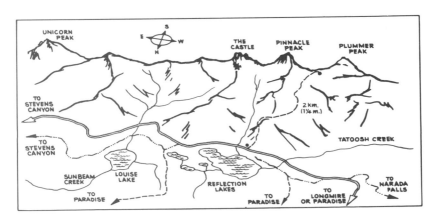

Mount Rainier from Pinnacle saddle

43 PARADISE FLOWER TRAILS

At Paradise the alpine fields achieve a climax unsurpassed anywhere in the Cascades. The flower season generally lasts from mid-July to mid-September, peaking the first of August. All are easily reached on paved trails. Drive to the large parking lot near the Paradise Ranger Station, elevation 5420 feet, and choose your trail for the day.

Flower Trails

Round trip 1–3 miles
Hiking time 1–3 hours
Elevation gain 500 feet

Snow doesn't leave the meadows until mid-July, but even in June flowers bloom on exposed ridges, including a large field of yellow glacier lilies on the south side of Alta Vista. A few days after the snow melts away the meadows turn white again with avalanche lilies, then blue with lupine and red with Indian paintbrush. In August the vast carpets of color yield to patches of asters, gentians, and many other flowers. In September the meadows turn a brilliant red.

Trails radiate from the Visitor Center, Paradise Inn, and the ranger station. All are good.

Nisqually Vista

Round trip 1¼ miles (2 km)
Hiking time 1 hour
Elevation gain 200 feet on return

Find the trail in the west parking lot 300 feet from the Visitor Center. The beginning is on stone steps. At an intersection in a few feet, keep left.

In ¼ mile the trail drops to a glacier viewpoint on the edge of the can-

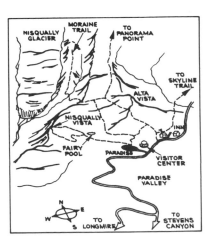

Snout of Nisqually Glacier as
photographed in 1968

Seed pod of the western anemone

yon. The glacier is descending from the summit like a slow-moving river. Snow accumulates at the higher elevations faster than it melts, growing hundreds of feet deep and compressing into ice pushing downhill at 10 or more inches a day. Some years the snout advances a few feet; other years it recedes. Compare the present position with the photograph on the opposite page taken in 1968.

Alta Vista

Round trip 1½ miles (2.5 km)
Hiking time 1½ hours
Elevation gain 500 feet

For both flowers and a view, the paved walk to the top of Alta Vista is especially recommended. Alta Vista is the green knoll directly above Paradise Inn.

Start at either the inn or near the ranger station and follow any of the many paved trails upward through the flower fields. The wide path which makes a switchback above the inn was, in Model T days, the road to Reeces' Camp in the Clouds, located in the trees to the side of Alta Vista. Whatever route is used, avoid the extremely steep trail that climbs directly up the face of Alta Vista. Go to the left, steeply for a short way then leveling off as the path contours around the backside to the top. Paradise Valley is laid out like a map with Mt. Adams and the Tatoosh Range across the way.

44 SKYLINE TRAIL

Loop trip 5 miles (8 km)
Hiking time 4 hours
High point 6900 feet

Elevation gain 1500 feet
Snowfree late July to mid-
October

Walk through meadows above the Nisqually Glacier to a high overlook of Paradise Valley with views of Mt. Adams, Mt. St. Helens, and Mt. Hood. A good place to watch avalanches in the Nisqually Icefall and marmots lazing in the sun.

Drive to the large parking lot near the Paradise Ranger Station, elevation 5420 feet. The trail starts on the stone steps left of the restrooms or in front of Paradise Inn.

The first ½ mile, paved, climbs steeply around the west side of Alta Vista. Beyond blacktop the way continues up the ridge toward the mountain. Bypass the signed "Glacier Vista"; a little farther up the trail, a bit more than 1 mile from the parking lot, is an even better look over the Nisqually Glacier. A long switchback leads to Panorama Point, aptly named.

Views of other volcanoes to the south open up beyond the Tatoosh Range. Mt. Adams, 45 miles to the southeast, has an appearance similar to Mount Rainier. The remnant of Mt. St. Helens' once symmetrical cone can be seen 46 miles to the southwest; before its 1980 eruption, the volcano looked remarkably like Japan's Fujiyama. On a clear day Mt. Hood, 96 miles away in Oregon, can be seen. To the east of Mt. Adams are Goat Rocks, the eroded roots of a once-mighty volcano.

From Panorama Point the trail crosses a short permanent snowfield, easy to traverse when the snow is soft, dangerous early in the morning or on a cloudy day when the snow is hard as ice. It then drops gradually 1 mile to the Golden Gate Trail (Hike 46), which can be used as a shorter alternate return to Paradise.

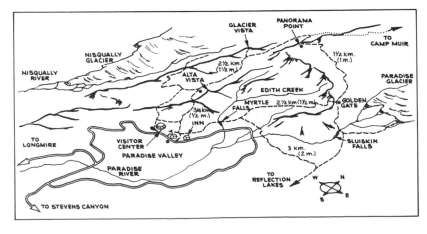

Tatoosh Range and Mount Adams from Panorama Point

The Skyline Trail continues ¾ mile down the ridge to the Stevens-Van Trump Memorial, where another trail branches off left to the Paradise Glacier (Hike 46). The Skyline Trail proceeds only a bit more along the ridge before dropping into Paradise Valley. A 300-foot climb from the valley to Myrtle Falls and a ½-mile paved trail complete the return to Paradise.

Until early August, at least, parts of the trail are covered by snow, requiring hiking boots—unlike the paved flower walks of Paradise.

45 CAMP MUIR

Round trip 9 miles (14½ km)
Hiking time 8 hours
High point 10,000 feet

Elevation gain 4600 feet
Recommended mid-July to
September

A long, arduous, and potentially hazardous ascent to the overnight cabin used by summit climbers. Climb through flowers, then rocks, then perpetual snow. At nearly 2 miles above sea level, look down on the Tatoosh Range, over the southern Cascade Mountains, and far into Oregon.

Take note: though hundreds of casual walkers go to Muir each year, this is not a trail hike. Much of the way is on snow. Part is over a permanent snowfield which is often crevassed in August and September. The mountain is notorious for "making its own weather"—mostly bad. On a clear day, without warning, clouds may form, enveloping hikers in blowing fog and wiping out all landmarks. At high elevation the temperature may fall abruptly, the wind rise, and a balmy afternoon turn swiftly into a killing night. (See the discussion of hypothermia in the Introduction.)

Drive to the large parking lot near the Paradise Ranger Station, elevation 5420 feet. Follow the Skyline Trail (Hike 44)1½ miles. On the side of the long switchback on Panorama Point, find the Pebble Creek trail, which climbs steeply beside a small creek. The sign says, "Camp Muir 2.7 miles." But don't feel too encouraged; for the average hiker, Muir is

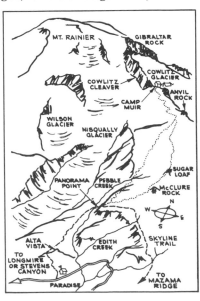

Climber above Camp Muir

Camp Muir, Cowlitz Glacier, and Gibraltar Rock

still 4 hours away. (The 2.7 miles must be "air miles." They couldn't be "as the crow flies" since even a bird would have to circle a few times to gain all that elevation.)

The trail continues ½ mile to Pebble Creek, a good spot to stop for a bite to eat. From here on there is no trail and the route is over steep, unbroken snowfields which can be hot and exhausting.

Head upward and slightly left over the Muir Snowfield toward Gibraltar Rock. Usually the snowfield is deeply covered in snow and perfectly safe, but some years crevasses open. Be wary of small surface cracks—they mark the location of holes that underneath may be very wide and very deep. Only an experienced mountaineer can tell which line of progress is safe—and when there are crevasses, only experienced mountaineers equipped with rope and ice axes should proceed. At such time hikers would be well advised to turn around; in any event they should follow only the well-used tracks and definitely give up if the snow is soft around the cracks.

The view from Camp Muir is very well worth the effort. A close-up look at the Cowlitz Glacier and the rubble wall of Gibraltar. Down below, a vertical 1 mile below, the tiny buildings at Paradise. Far off, more volcanoes—Mt. Adams and Mt. St. Helens, and a long way into Oregon, Mt. Hood and Mt. Jefferson.

Beargrass and Tatoosh Range from Paradise Glacier trail

PARADISE AREA

46   PARADISE GLACIER

Round trip 5½ miles (8¾ km)
Hiking time 3 hours
High point 6300 feet

Elevation gain 1100 feet
Snowfree late July through
   September

Hike through some of the finest flower fields in the Park, be whistled at by marmots, then climb to views above Paradise Valley and over the top of the Tatoosh Range to Mt. St. Helens and Mt. Adams. The trail ends on the barren moraines and remnants of the Paradise and Stevens Glaciers.

Drive to the large parking lot near the Paradise Ranger Station, elevation 5420 feet. The trail starts up the stone steps across from Paradise Inn, goes right, then on a paved path rounds a corner into flower fields of Edith Creek Basin and on to Edith Creek. Take the short side-trail to a spectacular view of Myrtle Falls and then cross Edith Creek. Beyond the bridge is a junction; keep right on the lower trail, which continues around the basin and drops 300 feet to a crossing of Paradise River. From here the trail climbs Mazama Ridge to a junction with the Lakes Trail (Hike 47). Stay left to the Stevens-Van Trump Memorial commemorating their (incomplete!) ascent of Mount Rainier in 1870. At the memorial is a junction with the Skyline Trail (Hike 44). Keep right along an old moraine. Much of this section will be across snow patches; follow the red posts. It is essential to stay on the trail; on each side there are dangerously steep snow slopes.

The Paradise and Stevens Glaciers were famous for their huge ice caves hollowed out by the action of water and wind. There may be small caves that develop in the future, but there is so little ice left that the big caves, for which Mount Rainier was so famous, will have to wait for the next ice age.

To see more country, either of two alternate return routes may be taken. For one, turn north (right) onto the Skyline Trail (Hike 44) at the Stevens-Van Trump Memorial, go ¾ mile and turn left at Golden Gate, descending into Edith Creek Basin and in 1½ miles rejoining the approach trail just above Myrtle Falls; this alternate is only ¼ mile longer than the approach, but requires several hundred feet of elevation gain to Golden Gate. For another return, almost 2 miles longer, continue on the Skyline Trail to Panorama Point and then back to the starting point.

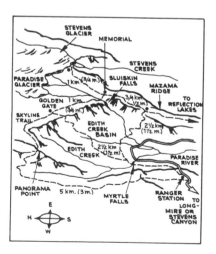

Marmot feeding in Edith Creek Basin

47 LAKES TRAIL

Loop trip via Reflection Lakes 4¾ miles (7½ km)
Hiking time 4 hours
High point 5800 feet

Elevation gain 1300 feet
Snowfree mid-July through September

Views, many small lakes, flowers, and forests on an up-and-down walk.

Drive to the large parking lot near the Paradise Ranger Station, elevation 5420 feet. The trail starts across the road from Paradise Inn or at the stone steps to the left of the restrooms. The beginning 1½ miles are identical with the Paradise Glacier trail (Hike 46).

The first ½ mile to Edith Creek is paved, traversing the hill above the inn. Cross the creek on the Myrtle Falls bridge. Keep right at the junction with the Skyline-Golden Gate Trail. The way traverses a bit higher, drops to a crossing of the Paradise River, and ascends switchbacks to Mazama Ridge. At a junction on the crest, turn right and leave the Paradise Glacier trail, following Mazama Ridge down from immense fields of flowers into alpine forest, passing numerous lakelets to a junction with an alternate section of the Wonderland Trail. Turn right, traversing slopes 500 feet above Reflection Lakes with views of the Tatoosh Range and the lakes, and in 1½ miles rejoin the Lakes Trail. Turn right, dropping to the Paradise River, crossing first the highway and then the river and finally climbing back to Paradise Valley. Join the Paradise-Longmire trail a short way below the parking lot.

For a slightly longer trip, with spectacular views of Mount Rainier and Reflection Lakes, continue on the Mazama Ridge trail to Faraway Rock and tiny Artist Pool. From the brink of steep slopes beside the pool look out to the Tatoosh Range and down to the lakes. Directly below is Louise

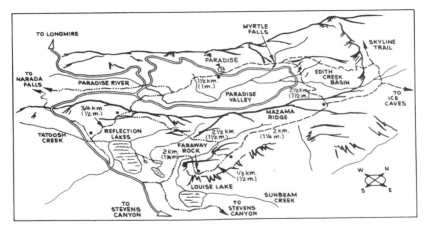

Avalanche lilies on Mazama Ridge

Lake. On a bench above the switchbacks on the Stevens Canyon Road is Bench Lake. To the right are Reflection and Little Reflection Lakes.

The trail descends abruptly to Little Reflection Lake. Walk along the shoulder of the road and pick up the Lakes Trail again at the first grove of trees by Reflection Lake. At the west shore is a junction. Keep right, climbing a low ridge to the rejoining of the Wonderland Trail and the return to Paradise.

48 PARADISE RIVER

One-way trip from Paradise to Longmire 6 miles (9½ km)	Recommended July through September
Hiking time 2½ hours	Recommended from Narada Falls
High point 5420 feet	June through October
Elevation loss 2700 feet	

Start in alpine meadows, descend into forest, pass two waterfalls, and end up walking along the Nisqually River.

The trip can be done in either direction, of course, but is most appealing when a party arrives at Paradise and finds the weather too poor or the snow too deep for high-country strolls. In such case don't give up the day as a lost cause: take the downhill trail either from Paradise or Narada Falls and finish either at Cougar Rock Campground or Longmire. Obviously a member of the group must be willing to drive the car down; either that or someone must arrange a ride back to where the car was left.

Drive to the large parking lot near Paradise Ranger Station, elevation 5420 feet. (Don't confuse this with the large, modern Paradise Visitor Center.) The trail begins on the south side of the lot, just where it funnels into the one-way downhill road.

In ½ mile is a junction to the Wonderland Trail and Lakes Trail (Hike 47); keep right, descending along the Paradise River. Cross the river at Stevens Canyon Road and soon reach the Narada Falls parking lot, 1¼ miles from Paradise.

Find the paved trail, marked "Narada Falls Viewpoint," which drops rapidly within sight, sound, and spray of the falls.

The paved trail ends at the viewpoint and a fork. Continue about 500 feet to the Wonderland Trail junction. Left are Reflection Lakes; go right, toward Longmire. In about 1 mile from Narada Falls is a bridge over the Paradise River and at about 1½ miles, two others over small creeks. Just before the first bridge is Paradise River Camp. The altitude is now 3800 feet and large Douglas firs appear amid the forest. At ap-

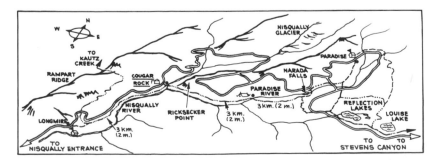

Wonderland Trail along the Nisqually River

proximately 2 miles cross the wooden pipeline that used to divert water to the Park's power generator. Watch for Carter Falls on the left, hidden behind a curtain of small trees. The next ¾ mile of trail more or less parallels the huge, wooden water pipes; the figures painted on trees at intervals note the number of feet from the generator.

The valley levels off rather abruptly. South are the towering cliffs of Eagle Peak; to the north is Ricksecker Point. The trail follows the service road about ¼ mile, crossing the Nisqually River close to the Paradise highway and the entrance to Cougar Rock Campground, 4 miles from Narada Falls.

To complete the remaining 2 miles to Longmire, don't cross the highway. Find the trail near the road and continue on downhill, sometimes in sight of the river, always in pleasant moss-covered forest.

49 VAN TRUMP PARK

Round trip 6 miles (10 km)
Hiking time 4 hours
High point 5800 feet

Elevation gain 2200 feet
Snowfree mid-July to mid-
    October

One of the most beautiful waterfalls in the Park, flower-strewn meadows, a look at the Kautz Glacier, and a better-than-average chance to see mountain goats—for such reasons this ranks among Rainier's most popular hikes.

Drive 10 miles from the Nisqually Entrance toward Paradise. The trail starts from a small parking lot on the left side of the road (elevation 3600 feet) ¼ mile before Christine Falls bridge.

To the crossing of Van Trump Creek the way is quite steep; beyond, only fairly steep. In ½ mile the trail traverses the first of three avalanche slopes where snowslides annually tear out parts of the tread; the passage can be dangerous early in the season when the trail is buried under a snowfield ending in wild water of the creek; it can also be dangerous after dark, even without snow.

At 1½ miles the track crosses a fork of Van Trump Creek and soon comes in sight of Comet Falls, 320 feet of thunder and mist. The best view is from the first two switchbacks—of the many which begin here.

Steep walking through trees and cliffs ends suddenly at the edge of the flower fields of Van Trump Park (2½ miles) and a junction.

The best view of Kautz Glacier is straight ahead on Mildred Point, a mile farther. However, the crossing of Van Trump Creek is very difficult until midsummer, so at the junction go right, climbing steeply a long ¼ mile to a 5800-foot viewpoint.

If transportation can be arranged, a loop trip can be made by returning down the Rampart Ridge trail 2½ miles to the Wonderland Trail junction. Take the left fork 1½ miles down to Longmire (Hike 3).

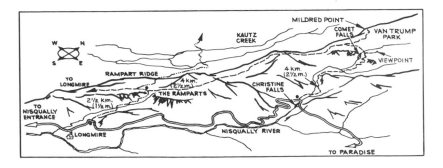

Comet Falls, 320 feet high

50 THE WONDERLAND TRAIL

Complete loop 93 miles (155 km)
Total elevation gain 20,000 feet
(6100 meters)

Snowfree mid-July through
August

The 93-mile Wonderland Trail completely encircling Mount Rainier was built in 1915 during an era when men were in a hurry and didn't mind steep walking. The trail passes through every life zone of the National Park from valley forests to alpine meadows to high barrens of rock and snow. Along the way are trees, flowers, animals, and glaciers. And views: so different does Rainier look from various segments, it's difficult to recognize it as all the same mountain. As the summit of Rainier is to a climber, so the Wonderland Trail is to a hiker—the experience of a lifetime.

A strong hiker can do the entire trail in a single week, but 10–14 days are about average and much more enjoyable. To allow full appreciation of scenic highlights and opportunity for side-trips, a party should spend 2 weeks or more—not forgetting extra time for sitting out several or so days of rain. Other hikers spread the hike over 2 or 3 years, hiking just a portion of the trail for a week each year. In each case, transportation must be arranged to avoid doubling back.

Supplies for the entire trip can be carried from the beginning, but this makes for hard, slow walking the early days. A better plan is to deposit food caches beforehand at two automobile-accessible intermediate points

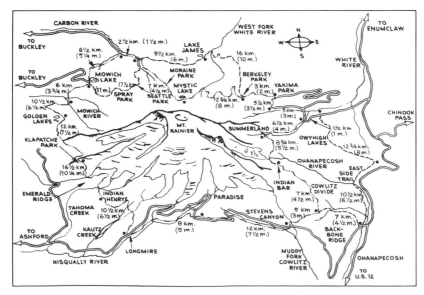

Wonderland Trail at Sunrise

around the circle, or arrange to be met at those points by friends bringing the supplies. Ranger stations will store food for you but cannot store any type of fuel. Longmire, Sunrise, and Paradise Ranger Stations are regularly manned during the summer season and open during normal business hours. However, other ranger stations, such as Mowich Lake and White River, are open only at irregular hours and some days not at all.

There is no place along the route to buy staples except the concession

Deer in silver forest along the trail to Golden Lakes

at Longmire; meals can be purchased at Sunrise, Paradise, and Long-mire for a change from backpack menus.

Be prepared for rain by carrying a tent or tarp. Few parties are lucky enough to complete the entire trip without a few days of mist, downpour, or perhaps snow—which can and does fall on the high meadows through-out the summer. The few, small shelter cabins cannot be counted on; they are frequently reserved for groups. Other details of equipment and plan-ning are covered in the Introduction.

Camping along the Wonderland Trail is allowed **only** at designated backcountry campsites and only with a backcountry camping permit for each night. (Experienced hikers may prefer the alternative "cross-country camping." Ask the rangers; they can advise you.)

There are 22 designated campsites, including 4 campgrounds reached by car. However, since campsites are not evenly spaced at 9- to 10-mile intervals (what the average hiker covers each day), some days a hiker may wish to cover 13–14 miles, passing several campsites. When plan-ning the itinerary and judging where to camp, take into consideration the elevation gains between campsites as well as the distances.

In applying for a permit, list every camp you plan to use and the dates. If unable to keep to schedule, contact the backcountry ranger for help to change your itinerary. Because backcountry campsites are limited, hikers are urged to start in midweek to assure camping spots.

The Wonderland Trail is described here starting at Longmire solely because that point has bus service; no need to drive your car from Chicago to do this American classic. There is no best starting point; they are all good. It makes no difference which way one hikes the Wonderland Trail, counterclockwise or, as described here, clockwise. The views are great no matter which way the eyes are pointed.

Part 1: Longmire to Mowich Lake

One-way trip 32½ miles (52 km)   Elevation gain 9900 feet
Allow 4–7 days   Snowfree mid-July through Sep-
High point 5900 feet   tember

The Wonderland Trail begins in forest and climbs to meadows—passing close to the Tahoma and Puyallup Glaciers, dips into trees and rises into flowers, again and again, and traverses the entire west side of The Mountain. There are seven campsites, at 3 miles, 5 miles, 11 miles, 14½ miles, 17¼ miles, 22¼ miles and 29 miles. Before starting, make certain you can handle the suspension bridge at Tahoma Creek (see comments in Hike 5); there is no alternate route.

From Longmire it is a short 3-mile climb over Rampart Ridge to Pyramid Creek Campground for an elevation gain of 1400 feet and a loss of 300 feet. *From Pyramid Creek* the next campsite at Devils Dream Creek is only 2 miles farther and 1000 feet higher. *From Devils Dream* it is 6 difficult but scenic miles to South Puyallup River Camp, as the Wonderland Trail climbs into the flower fields of Indian Henry's Hunting Ground (Hike 5) and drops 1700 feet to the dancing Tahoma Creek suspension bridge. From the bridge, the Wonderland Trail climbs 1400 feet over the prow of Emerald Ridge (Hike 7) and descends to the South Puyallup River Campsite. Total elevation gain, 2100 feet, with a loss of 2900 feet. *From South Puyallup River Camp* the way climbs steeply to meadowland, skirts St. Andrew's Lake, and still in meadows descends to Aurora Lake in Klapatche Park (Hike 8) and the most beautiful campsite on the trail, a distance of only 3½ miles from the South Puyallup

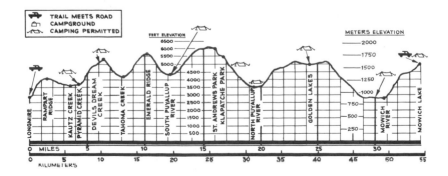

Berkeley Park

River and an elevation gain of 1900 feet and a loss of 400 feet. *From Klapatche Park* the trail goes back into forest, losing another 1900 feet in 2¾ miles to the North Puyallup River Campsite. From the river the trail climbs again into parkland to Golden Lakes Campsite in Sunset Park (Hike 9), a distance of 5 miles with an elevation gain of 1200 feet and a loss of 200 feet.

From Golden Lakes the Wonderland Trail leaves meadowland and descends into woods to Mowich River Campsite 6¾ miles from Golden Lakes with an elevation loss of 2400 feet. *From Mowich River* the trail climbs 2300 feet in 3½ miles to Mowich Lake.

Part 2: Mowich Lake to White River

One-way trip 30½ miles (49 km)
Allow 3–6 days
High point 6700 feet

Elevation gain 5200 feet
Snowfree mid-July through September

The second and most remote section of the Wonderland Trail rounds the cold north side of The Mountain, passing under looming Willis Wall and through flower meadows on the slopes of small peaks. There are six backcountry campsites along this section, at 5¼ miles, 8¼ miles, 12½ miles, 16 miles, 21½ miles, and 27½ miles.

From Mowich Lake to Ipsut Creek Campground the trail is fairly level to Ipsut Pass and then drops steeply to the campground (Hike 15), an easy and quick 5¼ miles with plenty of time for a side-trip to Eunice Lake and Tolmie Peak (Hike 11). However, there is a more strenuous but very rewarding alternate route to Carbon River by way of Spray Park (Hike 12) and Seattle Park (Hike 16), traversing miles of alpine flower fields before descending to the Carbon River Backcountry Campsite, with an elevation gain of 1700 feet and a loss of 3200 feet in 8 miles. The hike could be broken at either Eagle Roost or Cataract Valley Campsite along the way.

From Ipsut Creek Campground, the Wonderland Trail goes up the Carbon River Valley 3 miles (see Hike 17) and joins the alternate route at the Carbon River Campsite. *From Carbon River Campsite* it crosses a bouncy suspension bridge. (If the bridge worries you, see Hike 13 for an alternate route.) Leaving the bridge the trail climbs past the snout of the Carbon Glacier to Dick Creek Campsite, a long 4¼ miles (an elevation gain of 1800 feet) from Ipsut Creek. *From Dick Creek* the trail enters flower gardens with a great view of Willis Wall and descends 300 feet to Mystic Camp, 3¾ miles from Dick Creek. *From Mystic Camp* the next campsite is 5½ miles down past the snout of the Winthrop Glacier to Granite Creek, an elevation loss of 900 feet and a gain of 1100 feet. *From Granite Creek* the next campsite is 6 miles at Sunrise's walk-in campground. To reach it, the trail climbs 500 feet over Skyscraper Pass, traverses meadowland to Frozen Lake, and then drops to the campground. An alternative for those looking for an ice-cream cone or a hot meal is to go directly to the concession near the Sunrise parking area. Whichever trail is used, *from Sunrise* the Wonderland Trail drops 2000 feet in 3 miles to the White River Campground.

Note: Winthrop Creek bridge below the Winthrop Glacier is gone. Check with ranger for crossing difficulties.

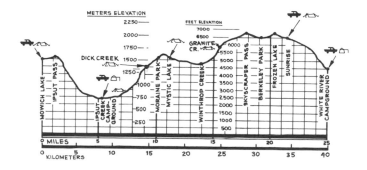

Martha Falls

Part 3: White River to Longmire

One-way trip 31 miles (50 km)
Allow 4–6 days
High point 6700 feet

Elevation gain 5700 feet
Snowfree mid-July through September

The third and final section of the Wonderland Trail, around the east side of The Mountain and back to the starting point on the south, offers still more forests, creeks, flowers, and glaciers. It traverses the highest portion of the circuit, the most likely place of all to see mountain goats.

There are five backcountry campsites along the way, at approximately 7 miles, 11½ miles, 16 miles, 19½ miles, and 27½ miles.

From White River Campground it is necessary to walk the campground road down to the paved Sunrise road. Go right, cross the highway bridge, and walk another 300 feet to the Wonderland Trail, paralleling the highway and then turning away and uphill, gaining 2100 feet in 4 miles, to campsites at Summerland (Hike 21), 7 miles from the start at White River. *From Summerland* it is another 4½ miles to campsites at Indian Bar. On the way cross high, barren Panhandle Gap (Hike 21) with a long traverse through a boulder field and snowpatches that may last through the summer, then descend to Indian Bar, an elevation gain of 800 feet and a loss of 1500 feet. If the weather is bad, one may want to consider staying an extra day at Summerland. (If party inexperience or wintry conditions make it necessary or desirable to avoid Panhandle Gap, an alternate route runs from Fryingpan Creek to Box Canyon via Owyhigh

Lakes, Hike 20; the East Side Trail, Hike 34; and Cowlitz Divide, Hike 39. Camps near Owyhigh Lakes and Deer Creek.)

From Indian Bar the next campsite is at Nickel Creek, 4½ miles, an elevation gain of 500 feet and a loss of 2300 feet. *From Nickel Creek* the trail crosses the Stevens Canyon Road and in 3½ miles reaches Maple Creek Camp, losing 800 feet. *From Maple Creek* the next step is 8 miles, gaining 2200 feet and losing 900 feet, a long, arduous and not exactly pleasant hike to Paradise River Campsite. Make an early start: the heat can be unbearable; even in morning shadows the heat of the day before radiates from the barren, burned-off canyon wall. Maybe the worst thing for morale is the stream of automobiles speeding along the Stevens Canyon Road, never out of sight or sound. Still, there are rewards. Sylvia Falls is a nice surprise, and so is cool and refreshing Martha Falls— actually a series of falls (the most interesting one is 300 feet above the trail). From Martha Creek the trail ascends another steep mile, crosses the road, and climbs on to Louise Lake and Reflection Lakes. From the lakes a hiker has a choice. One alternative is to follow the Wonderland Trail above Reflection Lakes, turning left just past Faraway Rock, proceeding over Mazama Ridge to Paradise Valley, crossing the Paradise River, and joining the Paradise-Longmire trail (Hike 48) ½ mile below Paradise. For the hiker so inclined, this is the place for a side-trip to Paradise Inn for ice cream, a steak, a bath, and a soft bed with clean sheets. The shorter alternative, and most practical, is to hike the road 1 mile from Reflection Lakes to the Paradise-Longmire trail. Drop along Paradise River below Narada Falls to Paradise River Camp.

The last section *from Paradise Camp* is an easy 3½ miles, all downhill, losing 1200 feet to Longmire. The trail follows the river under Ricksecker Point, crosses the Nisqually River near Cougar Rock Campground, and continues down to complete the loop at Longmire.

The hiker who arrives back at Longmire, having hiked 93 miles plus side-trips, having gained some 20,000 feet or more, can feel proud. The accomplishment is as impressive as climbing to the summit of Rainier. In many ways the hiker has come to know The Mountain more intimately than any climber and will be most aware of the many ways in which man and the mountain and its plants and animals are interrelated. The hiker will find, as John Muir did, that, "When we try to pick out anything by itself, we find it hitched to everything else in the universe."

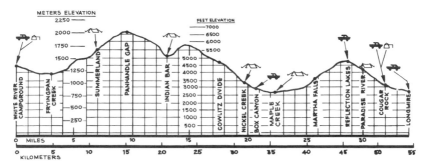

RECOMMENDED READING

Trips and Trails, 2: Family Camps, Short Hikes and View Roads in the Olympics, Mt. Rainier and South Cascades (third ed.), E.M. Sterling and Bob and Ira Spring. The Mountaineers, Seattle; 1983.

Geology of Mount Rainier National Park, Washington, Richard S. Fiske, Clifford A. Hopson, and Aaron C. Waters. Geological Survey Professional Paper 444. United States Government Printing Office, Washington; 1963.

Cascade Alpine Guide, Columbia River to Stevens Pass (second ed.), Fred Beckey. The Mountaineers, Seattle; 1986.

Mountaineering: The Freedom of the Hills (fourth ed.), Ed Peters, ed. The Mountaineers, Seattle; 1982.

Backpacking: One Step at a Time, Harvey Manning. Random, New York; 1981.

The Challenge of Rainier (third ed.), Dee Molenaar. The Mountaineers, Seattle; 1979.

The Story Behind the Scenery. K.C. Publications, Inc., Las Vegas; 1984.

Visitor's Guide to Glaciers of Mount Rainier National Park, Carolyn Priedger, Pacific Northwest National Parks and Forest Association, Seattle; 1985.

RECOMMENDED HIKING SEASONS

The recommended time of the year for hiking a particular trail is when the trail is generally free of snow. From year to year this varies a week or more; for a few weeks after the recommended time, snow patches can be expected on the trail. Above 5000 feet snowstorms occur quite frequently until mid-July and after late August and occasionally in between. However, midsummer snow usually melts in a few hours or a day.

MARCH–NOVEMBER
2   Longmire Woods Trails
13 Carbon River Trails

SNOWFREE IN MAY
3   Rampart Ridge (first mile)
4   Kautz Creek (first mile)
10 Paul Peak Trail
14 Green Lake
26 Huckleberry Creek
    (lower portion)
36 Laughingwater Creek Trail
    (first mile)
37 Grove of the Patriarchs
    (walk road to trailhead)
38 Silver Falls
48 Longmire to Carter Falls
    (first mile)

JUNE
6   Lake George
13 Carbon Glacier Viewpoint
15 Ipsut Creek
31 Crystal Lakes
34 East Side Trail

EARLY JULY
1   Eagle Peak Saddle
6   Gobblers Knob
7   Emerald Ridge
9   Sunset Park
    and Golden Lakes
20 Owyhigh Lakes
21 Summerland
22 Glacier Basin
35 Shriner Peak
36 Laughingwater
    Creek Trail

39 Cowlitz Divide
41 Bench and Snow Lakes
43 Nisqually Vista
48 Paradise to Longmire

MID-JULY
4   Kautz Creek
5   Indian Henry's Hunting Ground
8   Klapatche Park
11 Tolmie Peak
12 Spray Park
16 Seattle Park
17 Moraine Park-Mystic Lake
18 Windy Gap-Natural Bridge
19 Northern Loop Trail
23 Palisades Lakes
24 Sunrise Nature Trails
25 Sourdough Trail
26 Huckleberry Creek (top)
27 Mt. Fremont Lookout
28 Grand Park
29 Skyscraper Pass
32 Naches Peak Loop
33 Pacific Crest Trail-Dewey Lakes
40 Indian Bar
43 Paradise Flower Trails
44 Skyline Trail
45 Camp Muir
46 Paradise Glacier
47 Lakes Trail
49 Van Trump Park
50 Wonderland Trail

AUGUST
30 Burroughs Mountain
42 Pinnacle Saddle

INDEX

Other books from The Mountaineers include:

50 HIKES IN OREGON'S COAST RANGE AND SISKIYOUS

Rhonda and George Ostertag. Description of hikes in the mountain corridor between I-5 and Highway 101, including routes ranging from ½-mile walks to 47-mile backpacks.

55 HIKES IN CENTRAL WASHINGTON

Ira Spring, Harvey Manning. Route directions and descriptions for dayhikes and backpacks in the region from Wenatchee east to the Umatilla National Forest and from Lake Chelan south to the Columbia River.

100 HIKES Series:
WASHINGTON'S ALPINE LAKES REGION, Ira Spring, Vicky Spring, Harvey Manning.
WASHINGTON'S NORTH CASCADES: GLACIER PEAK REGION (Darrington-Monte Cristo, Glacier Peak Wilderness, Stevens Pass, Lake Wenatchee, Entiat), Ira Spring, Harvey Manning.
INLAND NORTHWEST, Rich Landers, Ida Rowe Dolphin.
WASHINGTON'S NORTH CASCADES NATIONAL PARK REGION (Mt. Baker Area, North Cascades National Park, Ross Lake National Recreation Area, Pasayten Wilderness, Methow-Chelan), Ira Spring, Harvey Manning.
OREGON, Rhonda & George Ostertag.
WASHINGTON'S SOUTH CASCADES & OLYMPICS, Ira Spring, Harvey Manning.

ADVENTURES IN IDAHO'S SAWTOOTH COUNTRY:
63 Trips for Hikers & Mountain Bikers

Lynne Stone. Guide to hiking and biking trails near Sun Valley, Ketchum, Hailey, and Stanley area.

BEST HIKES WITH CHILDREN
in Western Washington & the Cascades, Vol. 1 and 2

Joan Burton, Ira Spring. Complete details in two volumes on more than 175 different trips selected for particular appeal for children under 12. Mostly day hikes, from one to six miles round trip, which also offer camping possibilities.

CROSS-COUNTRY SKI ROUTES
of Oregon's Cascades: Mt. Hood, Bend

Klindt Vielbig. Details and maps on 197 tours, loops and connector trails, from beginner to intermediate levels.

CROSS COUNTRY SKI TOURS 1
Washington's North Cascades
CROSS COUNTRY SKI TOURS 2
Washington's South Cascades and Olympics

Vicky Spring, Tom Kirkendall. Details, maps and photos on more than 60 tours in each volume, for every level of cross-country skier from beginner to expert.

EXPLORING IDAHO'S MOUNTAINS
A Guide for Climbers, Scramblers, and Hikers

Tom Lopez. Route directions and descriptions for more than 700 summits in Idaho.

EXPLORING OREGON'S WILD AREAS
A Guide for Hikers, Backpackers, Cross Country Skiers & Paddlers

William L. Sullivan. Detail-stuffed guidebook to Oregon's 65 wilderness areas, wildlife refuges, nature preserves and state parks.

EXPLORING WASHINGTON'S WILD AREAS
Marge and Ted Mueller. Guide to 55 Washington State wilderness areas with outstanding recreational opportunities.

EXPLORING WASHINGTON'S WILD OLYMPIC COAST
David Hooper. Detailed information about hiking the beaches of Olympic National Park in Washington State.

MOUNT ST. HELENS National Volcanic Monument

Chuck Williams. A pocket-sized handbook for hikers, viewers and skiers that tells where visitors can drive and hike to best view the volcano and enjoy the Monument.

OLYMPIC MOUNTAINS TRAIL GUIDE
Robert L. Wood. Fully detailed guide to every trail in the Olympic National Park and Olympic National Forest, including scenic and historic highlights.

THE AFOOT & AFLOAT Series
    MIDDLE PUGET SOUND & HOOD CANAL
    NORTH PUGET SOUND
    THE SAN JUAN ISLANDS
    SOUTH PUGET SOUND

Marge and Ted Mueller. Water-based outdoor recreation guides to beaches, boating facilities, parks, landmarks, marine life on the shores and islands, for hikers, boaters, bicyclists and car travelers.

BEST SHORT HIKES Series
    IN WASHINGTON'S NORTH CASCADES & SAN JUAN ISLANDS
    IN WASHINGTON'S SOUTH CASCADES & OLYMPICS
E.M. Sterling. Day-long and shorter hikes for residents and visitors.

VISITORS' GUIDE TO THE ANCIENT FORESTS OF WESTERN
WASHINGTON

The Dittmar Family. Guidebook to 32 hikes in old-growth forests of the
Olympic Peninsula, North, Central, and South Cascades, and Puget Sound
region.

Send for illustrated catalog of more than 200 outdoor books published by:

The Mountaineers
1011 S.W. Klickitat Way, Suite 107, Seattle WA 98134